(Pictorial Press)

TOWARDS A NEW SOCIETY
Published in association
with NEW SOCIETY
Series Editor: PAUL BARKER

ANN OAKLEY
Sex, Gender, and Society

HARPER COLOPHON BOOKS
Harper & Row, Publishers
New York, Evanston,
San Francisco, London

SEX, GENDER AND SOCIETY was first published in 1972 by
Maurice Temple Smith Ltd, London in the series TOWARDS A NEW
SOCIETY. This series is published in association with NEW SOCIETY;
but the opinions expressed are the responsibility of the author and
do not commit the magazine as such in any way.

First HARPER COLOPHON edition published 1972

LIBRARY OF CONGRESS CATALOG CARD NUMBER: 72-9006

STANDARD BOOK NUMBER: 06-090320-1

Contents

SEX '...the two divisions of...human beings respectively designated as male or female'

GENDER '...any of two or more subclasses...that are partly arbitrary, but also partly based on distinguishable characteristics such as...sex, (as masculine, feminine...)'

SOCIETY '...an enduring and cooperating social group whose members have developed organised patterns of relationship through interaction with one another...a broad grouping of people having common traditions... collective activities and interests'

from Webster's Third New International Dictionary

Introduction

Everybody knows that men and women are different. But behind this knowledge lies a certain uneasiness: *how* different are they? What is the extent of the difference? What significance does it have for the way male and female behave and are treated in society?

While the first questions are factual ones, the last is a question of value. In practice, of course, fact and value are not always separated, and the confusion between them has been crucial in the debate about sex differences.

This debate has been carried on much more keenly during some historical periods than others. It seems to be revived at times when the existing roles and statuses of male and female are changing, and three periods in particular stand out: the century from about 1540 to 1640, the Victorian era, and the present time. In the last two, distinct 'women's movements' have arisen, and their existence suggests that, since the seventeenth century and the growth of industrialisation, basic issues to do with the role of women have never been solved.

In the period from 1540 to 1640, women were certainly on the defensive over their rights in society but it was a matter of maintaining these rights rather than obtaining them. A great deal of practical equality between the sexes had evolved by that time, particularly in the commercial field, and the woman who traded in her own right (as many did) was given as much freedom and responsibility as a man. If the law did not allow this, custom did, and custom was a much more binding influence on people's behaviour than it is now.

This equality of male and female was seen both as a threat—a crime against nature—and as a moral and natural right. Those who looked upon it as a threat, saw the similarity of male and female in behaviour, personality, gesture and dress as symbolic of a growing and catastrophic confusion in the social roles of the sexes. Those who applauded it perceived that equality was more important than the kind of short-term security gained by staying within the boundaries of sex roles in which male and female were opposed and different rather than equal and similar.

In 1620 two pamphlets appeared with titles which show this preoccupation with the interchangeability of role between male and female: 'Hic Mulier: Or, the Man-woman: Being a Medicine to cure the Coltish Disease of the Staggers in the Masculine-Feminines of our Times', and 'Haec Vir: Or the Womanish-Man'. The first pamphlet 'Hic Mulier' reads rather like a modern protest against the masculinity of liberated women; it was a criticism of the Elizabethan woman's independent behaviour, which many people feared would dissolve marital and domestic happiness. Such was the (predominantly male) fear of women's independence that a proclamation was issued in 1547 forbidding women 'to meet together to babble and talk' and ordering men, with more hope than realism, 'to keep their wives in their houses'. The tone of 'Hic Mulier' followed that of the 1547 edict, but the tone of 'Haec Vir' is strongly feminist: '...we are as freeborn as Men, have as free election and as free spirit, we are compounded of like parts, and may with like liberty make benefit of our creations.' The pamphlet urges that male and female deserve the same equal treatment, and that if women are treated unequally then this restriction of freedom amounts to slavery.

'Hic Mulier' and 'Haec Vir' were only two of the many publications that appeared between 1540 and 1640 on the subject of sex differences. Other titles included John Knox's 'The Monstrous Regiment of Women' and Robert Vaughan's 'A Dialogue in Defense of Women, against malicious detractors' (1542) which condemned, among other things, the double standard of morality. Probably one of the reasons for this interest in the relative merits of the sexes was the presence during most of the period of a woman on the throne. The mere fact of a female monarch seemed to suggest that women were worth more than some people thought they ought to be.

But of much greater significance was the emergence of a new commercialistic society, in which no rigid pre-existing doctrines dictated what the roles of the sexes should be. Political and social conditions focussed attention on the relationships between male and female by altering their relative statuses in practice. Significant ties with the past were severed: the break with medieval conventions in the late fifteenth and early sixteenth centuries vastly increased women's responsibilities; the break with Roman Catholicism led to the formation of new opinions on women, marriage and the home. The Roman Church's repressive attitude to sexuality diminished in influence, and although the Puritan attitude was later substituted, Puritanism was also allied with commercial success and with the doctrine of personal responsibility, fields in which women had already proved their abilities.

So the first Elizabethan era was a time of reappraisal, in which the relative worth of male and female became a topic of social relevance. The same kind of debate reappeared two centuries later, with the beginnings of the movement for 'emancipating' women. In between these two periods, those who argued in favour of sex differences had defeated the champions of women's rights; the roles of the sexes had become sharply separated, and along with this went a polarisation of male and female interests, activities and personalities. Woman's place in the new commercial society had turned out to be different from man's. Woman's place was in the home, and men were drawn outside it into factories (and later into offices) where 'work' became something divided from 'family', in contrast to the earlier unity between the two. As one historian has remarked, the doctrine that woman's place is in the home is the product of a period in which men had recently been displaced from it. (One wonders what might have happened if the industrial revolution had occurred at a time when women were not tied to the home by constant childbearing. In a climate of women's independence, with contraceptive efficiency lessening the impact of biology on social role, the split between work and home brought about by industrialisation might have had quite different consequences.)

Although women were not specifically excluded from the franchise until 1832, the erosion of their legal, political and economic position had begun in the sixteenth century, just at a time when writers of feminist pamphlets were arguing that nature, supported their notion of a sexually egalitarian society. By the time Mary Wollstonecraft produced that first, premature document of the Victorian debate, her 'Vindication of the Rights of Women' (1792), the emphasis on the assumed inferiority of women was pronounced. It was clear to everyone that women in society *were* inferior, and most people concluded that this inferiority began in nature and was therefore unalterable. In the mid-nineteenth century, Caroline Norton, who improved the status of women as mothers through her influence on the Custody of Infants Act (1839), spoke for many when she said with conviction 'I believe in the natural superiority of the man as I do in the existence of a God.' Mary Wollstonecraft, for her part, pointed out that the inferiority of women was a consequence (rather than a cause) of women's position in society, and that if people ceased believing in the inferiority of women, and acting according to this belief, then women might cease to be inferior. 'Let woman share the rights, and she will emulate the virtues of men.'

From about 1830 until the first decades of this century, the arguments for and against the equality of male and female concentrated largely on the discrimination created by particular social institutions. The female's exclusion from the franchise, her supposed inability to benefit from education, her legal status as a childlike dependent, parasitic on the goodwill of husband or father—these were the questions which occupied the attention of Wollstonecraft and her successors in the Victorian debate over sex differences. Their insistence on political rights arose out of the protest against domestic inequality: one supporter of feminism pointed out in 1825 that 'Home...is the eternal prison-house of the wife: the husband paints it as the abode of calm bliss, but takes care to find out of doors, for his own use, a species of bliss not quite so calm...The home is his home with everything in it, and of all the fixtures, the most abjectly his is his breeding machine, the wife.' The escape from domestic subjection, from the stereotype of the passive, obedient female, could only be obtained by the exercise of rights outside the home, so feminists argued.

Even among feminists, most people (including Mary Wollstonecraft) believed that nature dictated some sex differences whose social significance was obvious—'bodily strength' for example. Perhaps because the Victorian attitude towards women was so generally discriminatory and repressive, the attention of feminists concentrated on only some of the issues raised by it. Certainly the female claim to political and educational equality was given far more attention than was the general moulding of feminine (and masculine) personality by social convention—by the idea of 'the lady'. Mary Wollstonecraft's own attack on cultural femininity was not repeated with the same passion as the century wore on. The desires and achievements of the feminists centred on identifiable rights, rather than on the influence of less visible ideas and opinions. They worked for and obtained the extension of the concept of citizenship to women.

The emancipation of women was begun in an atmosphere sensitive to the plight of underpriviledged peoples. Parallels between the economic and emotional bondage of French peasants or American slaves and that of women, were constantly drawn and obviously relevant. The Victorian patriarchy was founded on ideas of supremacy similar to those attacked by the French revolution and in the abolition of slavery in America. What was in process of liberation was the concept of human individuality and its pre-eminence over all considerations of birth and fortune. As John Stuart Mill wrote in 'On the Subjection of Women' (1869), 'What, in unenlight-

13 ened societies, colour, race, religion or, in the case of

a conquered country, nationality, are to some men, sex is to all women; a peremptory exclusion from almost all honourable occupations.'

Mill argued for the treatment of women as individuals, but many people saw the application of this concept to women's status as a threat to marital happiness and to the whole basis of relationships between male and female—arguments with which the seventeenth century debater would have been very familiar. An antifeminist book published in 1831 reproduced the old argument that 'Nothing is so likely to conciliate the affection of the other sex as a feeling that women look to them for guidance and support'—a bad argument as applied to the status of women, though a slightly better one as applied to the goal of preserving the institution of Victorian marriage. People were worried, as they had been in the sixteenth and seventeenth centuries, that an extension of men's rights to women might fundamentally change existing definitions of masculinity and femininity. The more justification there was in the argument that women were conditioned by society, the more reasonable seemed the fear that emancipation would change society. And the more people wanted to keep society as it was, the more they opposed feminism.

The same pattern has appeared in our own time. Since the emancipation movement, the civil status of the sexes has become more nearly equal: in the eyes of the law, in the realm of political rights and duties, there are fewer sex differences than there have ever been since the emergence of industrialised society in the West. On the other hand, there have been, and still are, many attempts to belittle the twentieth-century achievement, by stressing the decline in personal happiness and the growth of social confusion that these changes in the status of the female are supposed to have brought about. These attempts, like the protests aired in the sixteenth and seventeenth centuries and in the Victorian period, are anxious and defensive reactions to threatened changes of sex roles.

The present-day women's liberation movement

does, on the other hand, have certain characteristics which separate it from the feminism of the two earlier periods. Today's liberationists point out that both men and women are caught in the web of conventional sex-role definition, and that both sexes may suffer from a restriction of personal freedom as a result—not just women. This is a new idea, due perhaps to the perception that conventional ideas about the roles of the sexes persist despite the removal of institutional restrictions on the freedom of women to behave 'like men'. This perception, together with the increasingly crucial economic importance of women, should lead us to look again, as dispassionately as we can, at the extent of the differences—and the similarities—between male and female.

The enduring questions are these: does the source of the many differences between the sexes lie in biology or culture? If biology determines male and female roles, how does it determine them? How much influence does culture have?

These questions are more meaningful now than they were in the previous debates about sex differences, for the simple reason that we are now able to disregard (if we wish) almost all the so-called consequences of the reproductive division between the sexes. Fertility control and the safe artificial feeding of infants enable couples to choose when they shall have babies, and who shall feed them. The former is an achievement of personal relevance for all women, while the latter is of potential (though usually underrated) relevance to both sexes, since it makes it possible to distribute both the work and the joy of childrearing between people regardless of their biological sex: that is, it could bring men back into the home.

However much we *could* change the traditional involvement of women with their biological roles, the direction of change remains a question of choice and of value. It is not enough to point out that the traditionally incontrovertible argument for the sex-differentiated society has had its foundations

removed with the advance of pills, loops, rubber
devices, synthetic human milk and sterilised feeding
bottles. Arguments long believed in have an alarming
tendency to remain suspended in thin air by the
slender string of passionate, often irrational,
conviction. They seem not to need their foundations
to survive.

Technology has altered the necessary impact of
biology on society, but our conceptions of masculinity and femininity have shown no corresponding
tendency to change. The lag between the two points
to a crucial distinction it is necessary to make in our
thinking about male and female roles—the distinction
between 'sex' and 'gender'. 'Sex' is a word that refers
to the biological differences between male and
female: the visible difference in genitalia, the related
difference in procreative function. 'Gender' however
is a matter of culture: it refers to the social classification into 'masculine' and 'feminine'.

The distinction between 'male' and 'female' on the
one hand, and 'masculine' and 'feminine' on the
other, makes it possible to clarify much of the
argument about sex differences. Just as seventeenth-
century titles like 'Hic Mulier' and 'Haec Vir' call for
this important distinction between sex and gender to
be made, so do twentieth-century titles like 'The
Feminised Male' and 'The Female Eunuch'. That
people are male or female can usually be judged by
referring to the biological evidence. That they are
masculine or feminine cannot be judged in the same
way: the criteria are cultural, differing with time and
place. The constancy of sex must be admitted, but
so also must the variability of gender. A failure to see
this has led to overstated arguments and distorted
conclusions. In fact prejudice has probably done
more to determine the social roles of the sexes than
biology ever could—and if 'prejudice' is what we
mean by culture, our pretences to enlightenment are
not worth a great deal.

As John Stuart Mill observed in 1869, the topic of
sex differences is one on which almost everybody
feels qualified to dogmatise, while 'almost all neglect

and make light of the only means by which any partial insight can be obtained into it.' What Mill meant was that people rarely refer to the evidence about the differences and similarities between male and female before pronouncing their conclusions. While deploring this tendency, he admitted that sound evidence on the subject was sadly lacking in his time: we need, he said, to study 'the laws of the influence of circumstances on character.'

The rise of the social sciences has, since Mill wrote, provided us with exactly this kind of evidence, and the examination of it is the substance of this book. Fundamentally, its task is to disentangle 'sex' from 'gender' in the many fields where the existence of natural differences between male and female has been proposed, aiming to replace dogmatism by insight, and attempting to separate value-judgments from statements of fact.

1

The biology of sex

The starting point for the study of sex differences is biology. But biology also demonstrates the *identity* of male and female—their basic similarities, the continuity in their development. Far from falling into two discrete groups, male and female have the same body ground-plan, and even the anatomical difference is more apparent than real. Neither the phallus nor the womb are organs of one sex only: the female phallus (the clitoris) is the biological equivalent of the male organ, and men possess a vestigial womb, whose existence they may well ignore until it causes enlargement of the prostate gland in old age.

What is 'sex'? How do the differences and similarities of the sexes arise? This chapter looks at the origin of sex differentiation in biology, and at some of its possible consequences in social life.

In ordinary usage the word sex has two meanings: it refers to the differences between individuals that make them male and female, and also to a type of behaviour—the 'mating' behaviour that begins sexual reproduction. Not all organisms, of course, do reproduce in this way; some reproduce asexually by releasing a cell or group of cells from one organism alone. In humans, reproduction is sexual because there is an exchange of nuclear cell material between different mating types—male and female. This process of exchanging and mixing genetic material is what biologists mean by 'sex'. In evolutionary terms, the division of a species into male and female has adaptive advantages: greater variation between individuals is possible, and genetic weaknesses can be bred out.

Both male and female, therefore, contribute genetic material in reproduction, but only one of them, the male, determines the sex of the child. It is a chromosome in his sperm that decides whether the new baby shall be male or female. The cells of the female ovary and male testis each contain twenty-three chromosomes in which all the genetic 'information' for the child is coded. One of the twenty-three is the sex chromosome and this can be of two types, X and Y. (They are so called because of their shape. The Y chromosome looks like an incomplete X and is one fifth of its size.) Female ova all contain only the X sex-determining chromosome, while male sperm carry either the X or the Y chromosome. When a Y sperm fertilises an ovum, the embryo will have the sex determination XY, which means that it will be male. If it is an X sperm, the embryo will be XX, female.

In this way the genetic or chromosomal sex of an individual is determined at conception. However, the differences between male and female anatomy are the product of nine months' gestation, and various hazards lie in wait for the developing embryo. Up to about seven weeks of prenatal life the appearance of the external genitalia is identical in both sexes. The basic plan of the development of the sex organs and ducts is common to males and females, and the same two sets of ducts develop in both.

At first there is a single external opening leading both to the bladder and to the internal genitalia (the urogenital opening) and a 'genital tubercle' which is the rudimentary penis or clitoris. After seven weeks the male ducts cease to develop in the female and the female ducts in the male. If the embryo is chromosomally male, the genital tubercle enlarges to form the penis while the urethra (the duct through which urine is discharged) extends so as to pass right through it. The skin round the urogenital opening unites to form the scrotum, into which the testes descend later, usually just before birth. If the embryo is chromosomally female, none of these changes occur: the genital tubercle atrophies and becomes the clitoris, the skin around the urogenital opening remains divided and becomes the labia. (See Figure 1.)

This period during which embryos differentiate into specifically male or female anatomical forms is obviously a critical one. Cases in which embryos develop either as incomplete males or as incomplete females are due to some failure in the critical early period. What makes this anatomical differentiation occur in the first place? How is the message of the

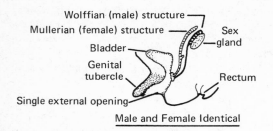

Wolffian (male) structure
Mullerian (female) structure
Sex gland
Bladder
Genital tubercle
Rectum
Single external opening

Male and Female Identical

Sexual organs of baby at 2nd to 3rd month of pregnancy

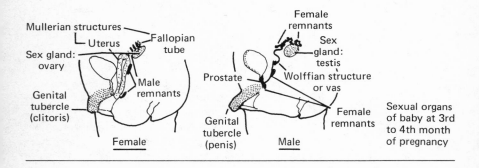

Mullerian structures
Uterus
Fallopian tube
Sex gland: ovary
Male remnants
Genital tubercle (clitoris)

Female

Female remnants
Sex gland: testis
Wolffian structure or vas
Prostate
Female remnants
Genital tubercle (penis)

Male

Sexual organs of baby at 3rd to 4th month of pregnancy

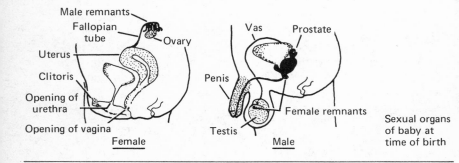

Male remnants
Fallopian tube
Ovary
Uterus
Clitoris
Opening of urethra
Opening of vagina

Female

Vas
Prostate
Penis
Female remnants
Testis

Male

Sexual organs of baby at time of birth

1(a) Differentiation of internal genitals in the foetus.

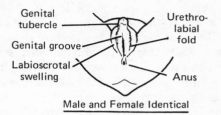

Genital
tubercle

Urethro-
labial
fold

Genital groove

Labioscrotal
swelling

Anus

Male and Female Identical

Sexual organs
of baby at 2nd
to 3rd month
of pregnancy

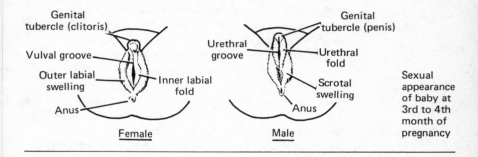

Genital
tubercle (clitoris)

Genital
tubercle (penis)

Vulval groove

Urethral
groove

Urethral
fold

Outer labial
swelling

Inner labial
fold

Scrotal
swelling

Anus

Anus

Female

Male

Sexual
appearance
of baby at
3rd to 4th
month of
pregnancy

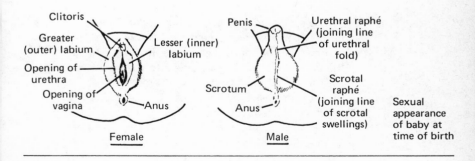

Clitoris

Penis

Urethral raphé
(joining line
of urethral
fold)

Greater
(outer) labium

Lesser (inner)
labium

Opening of
urethra

Scrotum

Scrotal
raphé
(joining line
of scrotal
swellings)

Opening of
vagina

Anus

Anus

Female

Male

Sexual
appearance
of baby at
time of birth

1(b) Differentiation of external genitals in the foetus.

chromosomes transmitted to the developing embryo? What happens (or fails to happen) in cases of imperfect sexual development? Despite recent research we are still very far from the answers.

It seems clear that, as one endocrinologist (S LeVine) has put it, the basic human form is female and masculinity comes about as the result of something 'added'. This conclusion has been reached as a result of several pieces of evidence, beginning with the solution of a problem that had puzzled cattle breeders for centuries—the problem of the 'freemartin', an intersexed calf. Freemartins are always born as the twin of a normal male and during pregnancy the placentas nourishing the two calves are joined. The freeemartin starts as a genetic female and is masculinised by hormones produced in the male calf and circulated to the freemartin through the connecting placental tissue. These hormones are produced by the gonads (testes) of the male, in both calf and human embryo, and they provide the added something which causes the embryo to develop in the male direction. The presence of the Y chromosome in the genetic make-up of the male somehow provokes the embryonic gonad into hormone production, whereas the XX combination has no such effect, and the female gonad (ovary-to-be) produces hormones only at a much later stage. Just how genes on the Y chromosome have this effect is not known.

The crucial role played by the gonadal hormones in initiating male development has been demonstrated by countless animal experiments. In several species the injection of male hormone into the female during the critical period completely reverses it sex. On the other hand, castrated embryos of either genetic sex develop into females, and this suggests that the role of the male hormone is a dual one: its presence ensures the development of male structures but it is also needed to prevent the development of female structures, which are capable of developing autonomously. For an embryo to develop as a female, its gonads do not need to produce female hormones. Normal sex differentiation depends exclusively on the presence or absence of the male hormone.

Further evidence of the importance of hormones in establishing anatomical sex differentiation is provided by studies of intersexuals. It can happen that an individual of one chromosomal sex develops the gonads of the opposite sex, and the hormones from these gonads produce a physical appearance as male or female quite unrelated to the chromosomal sex. One particular form of intersexuality, in which genetic males have male gonads but female secondary sex characteristics and female external genitalia, is thought to be due precisely to the failure of the male gonad to produce male hormones during the critical period of prenatal life. (The cause is probably a sex-linked recessive gene, carried by females and passed on to genetic males.)

The critical period is (fortunately perhaps) short—in the rabbit castration before embryonic day 21 causes complete female development of a genetic male, but castration at day 24 fails to interfere with normal male development. In humans, the critical period occupies the space of a few days late in the third prenatal month. After this time hormones have no basic irreversible effect.

Because of the importance of hormones in what follows, it will be as well to give here a brief account of their functions as they relate to sex differences.

The term 'hormones' covers all the secretions of the endocrine glands (the pituitary, the adrenal glands, the thyroid gland, the pancreas, the ovary and testis). The number and range of hormones produced by males and females is virtually the same, but normal women usually produce a preponderance of the female sex hormones, oestrogen and progesterone, the normal males a preponderance of testosterone and the general group of hormones known as androgens, or male sex hormones.

The sex hormones are produced not only by the ovary and testis but by the adrenal glands as well. This fact partially accounts for the male castrate's ability to maintain a 'normal' sex life despite his

23

sterility, and it also accounts for some cases in which genital appearance is contrary to chromosomal sex (a type of pseudo-intersexuality). Just as a male embryo whose gonads fail to function properly takes on female genital characteristics, so a female embryo can be born with male genital appearance if its adrenal glands produce an excess of androgenic hormones. Tumours in the adrenal glands of adults can be responsible for similar hormone reversals, producing changes in the appearance of secondary sex characteristics.

Methods of measuring the amount of hormones that individuals secrete are complicated by the ability of the body to manufacture male hormones from female hormones and vice versa. An injection of the male hormone testosterone may be partly converted by the body into its near chemical neighbour, the female hormone oestrogen. (This tendency is thought to explain, for instance, the fact that rapidly maturing male adolescents sometimes acquire small breasts-the substantial increase in testosterone which accompanies puberty is partially metabolised as oestrogen, which in turn causes breast development.)

Despite problems of measurement, there is good evidence that up to about eight or ten years of age, boys and girls secrete negligible amounts of the sex hormones. Thereafter, in both sexes, the production of both male and female hormones increases. With the approach of puberty the increase in the production of male hormones in *both* sexes becomes pronounced (it reaches a peak in the age range twenty to forty, when the difference between the hormones produced by men and women is also at its highest level). The increase in the female hormone is much greater for girls than boys, accelerating particularly around the age of eleven, and becoming cyclic about eighteen months before the onset of menstruation itself. But oestrogen production in boys does increase at puberty, although it never becomes cyclic—as androgen production in females never becomes cyclic either. (See Figure 2.)

While men and women produce both male and

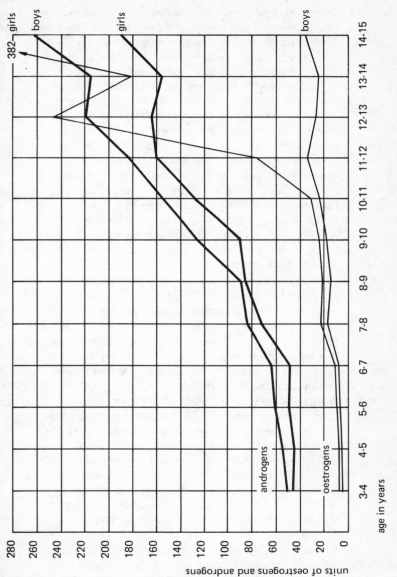

2 Production of male hormones (androgens) and female hormones (oestrogens) in boys and girls. The level of production is measured by the number of units excreted in the urine each day.

female hormones, the relative amounts and proportions vary a great deal between individuals and one cannot establish biological maleness or femaleness from the hormone count alone. In one study of two women and three men (all 'normal' individuals) the level of female hormones excreted in the urine was 155.2 and 13.4 units per day for the two women, and 12.4, 7.6 and 16.8 units for the three men. The production of male hormones varies in a similar way between individuals of the same and different sexes. Roger Williams in his 'Biochemical Individuality' suggests that it is possible to classify both men and women in nine categories according to their production of low, medium or high levels of male and female hormones (low androgen + low oestrogen, low androgen + medium oestrogen, and so on for all nine possible combinations). One would then find a mixture of both sexes in each of the categories over this range—although some might be more characteristically male than female, and vice versa.

The main function of the sex hormones in both male and female is to ensure that the body develops in line with its chromosomal sex and so becomes capable of reproduction. They have other functions too—some directly related to reproductive behaviour, some whose connection with reproduction is obscure. Male hormones encourage hair growth on the body, but are inversely related to hair growth on the scalp. A woman treated with testosterone for cancer of the breast may develop both hair on the face and the frontal baldness of the scalp which is a male characteristic. Conversely a man given oestrogen for cancer of the prostate may develop a female pattern of pubic hair and a slower growth of hair on the face.

The general growth and maturation of male and female are directly under the control of hormones. At puberty, the increase in growth in both sexes is caused by an increase in the production of androgens. But in girls the simultaneous rise in oestrogen production causes maturation or ossification of the bones, a process which, once completed, prevents further growth. Thus, because of the relatively low

level of oestrogen in their bodies, boys have a longer
time in which to grow before their bones mature. It
seems possible that the output of sex hormones
controls the secretion of the so-called 'growth'
hormone from the pituitary, but how it does this is
not known.

After puberty, the sexual function of oestrogen in
women seems to be limited to monitoring changes in
the womb related to menstruation, ovulation,
conception and gestation—and to keeping the vagina
in a state of lubricated receptivity. The amount of
oestrogen produced by a woman does not control her
sexual drive, erotic imagery or sensation, or her
ability to have an orgasm. After the menopause,
oestrogen production declines to a clinically
insignificant level but many women experience at
that time a new awakening of sexual desire. (It is
thought that this is due to release from the fear of
pregnancy.)

The later period of life brings the sexes closer
together in terms of hormone production. Around
the late fifties and early sixties both ovary and testis
start to produce radically smaller amounts of
hormones, so that in this way men and women revert
to the relatively neuter condition of childhood.

In those ways, chromosomes and hormones influence
the development of the sexes. What other sex
differences are determined by biology?

Genetic maleness is correlated not only with the
possession of penis and testicles, but also with greater
size, weight and strength. These are, in fact, the sum
total of the advantages produced by the Y chromosome.

At birth a male baby weighs more than a female
baby. The average weights (in pounds) are 7.50
(male) and 7.44 (female) in Caucasian infants; 6.49
(male) and 6.35 (female) in Indian infants; and 6.87
(male) and 6.72 (female) in Indonesian infants.
Heights also differ between the sexes: boy babies are
about one inch longer at birth than girls in Western
societies. In the sample of 5,386 children studied by

J W B Douglas and J M Blomfield, the average height of two-year-old boys was 33.7 inches and that of two-year-old girls 33.3 inches, rising to 40.7 and 40.4 inches respectively at the age of four and a quarter. This difference is an average one, and the vast majority of both boys' and girls' heights fall within the same range. (See Figure 3.) Height is also determined by social-environmental factors which can outweigh the sex difference, and the daughter of a professional worker is likely to be as tall as the son of an unskilled worker. The sex differential in height also varies between different populations. In one American Indian group the average difference in height between the sexes is less than two inches; in another it is six inches; an African Negro group shows an average difference of eight inches.

The sex difference in both height and weight may be related to food intake—in many societies the male traditionally takes the greater share of available food. This continues today; in Nigeria, for example, most, if not all, of the severe malnutrition cases seen by one British doctor in the period following the Biafran war in 1970 were female children. This doctor, Sylvia Watkins, wrote that 'if food is scarce, the boys are given what little there is, leaving the girls to starve. It was not uncommon to see whole families of girls with severe kwashiorkor [a protein deficiency disease] whilst the son and heir was fit and well.' In one such family, the two-year-old girl weighed 12 pounds while her five-month-old brother had reached 18 pounds. But males are not always the favoured ones. Margaret Mead described one tribe—the Mundugumor—where the women were as tall as the men; they also had all the food, doing all the fishing and eating any amount they chose before bringing the food supply to the men of the village.

In terms of somatotype (body physique) there are sex differences which are visible and accepted as standard in our own society. The more muscular physiques occur less often among girls, and there is some evidence that genes located on the X chromosome may somehow inhibit the development of large

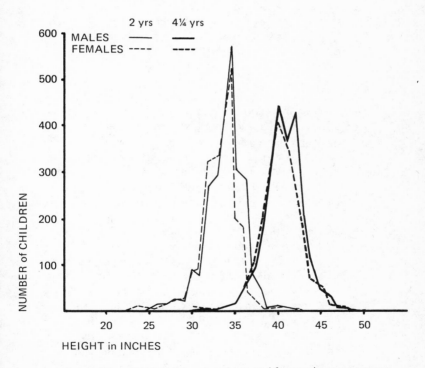

3 Heights of girls and boys aged two and four and a quarter years.

muscles. The relative proportions of body surface taken up by the trunk, head, limbs and so on, also differ between the sexes, with females tending to one mean and males to another.

Again the degree of difference between male and female somatotypes varies between ethnic groups. In one small-scale ('primitive') society for which there are good photographic records—the Manus of the Admiralty Islands—there is apparently no difference at all in somatotype between males and females as children, and as adults both men and women tend to the same high degree of mesomorphy (broad shoulders and chest, heavily muscled limbs, little subcutaneous fat) which is not found to the same extent in American and Western European groups. In Bali, too, males and females lack the sort of differentiation of physique that is a visible sex difference in our culture. Geoffrey Gorer once described them as a 'hermaphroditic' people; they have little sex differential in height and both sexes have broad shoulders and narrow hips. They do not run to curves and muscles, to body hair or to breasts of any size. (Gorer remarked that you could not tell male and female apart, even from the front.) Another source informs us that babies suck their fathers' breasts as well as their mothers'.

It is clear from all this that there is a great deal of cultural variation in the effect produced by the sex-determining chromosomes on secondary sex characteristics and general physique. The characteristics considered so far are those that tend to favour the male, but on the minus side the Y chromosome is responsible for a host of handicaps. The list given by Ashley Montagu in his book 'The Natural Superiority of Women' contains sixty-two specific disorders due largely or wholly to sex-linked genes and found mostly in males. About half of them are serious, and include haemophilia (failure of the blood clotting mechanism), mitral stenosis (a heart deformity) and some forms of mental deficiency. Others are relatively trivial, ranging from red-green colour blindness (which between 4 and 8% of all men have) to

Balinese girl   (Paul Popper)

the presence of a white lock of hair on the back of the head. The genes that cause these disorders are mutant ones. They are sex-linked because they are carried by the X chromosome, and in a female child the X chromosome inherited from the other parent counterbalances the effect of the mutant gene inherited from the first. The disorders are therefore due not so much to the presence of the Y chromosome as to the absence of the second X chromosome in males. Many other disadvantages of being male seem to have no known cause.

At every stage of life, beginning with conception, more genetic males die than genetic females. More males than females are produced, and the two facts of greater mortality and greater production seem to go hand in hand. Although X and Y sperms appear to be produced in equal numbers, between 120 and 150 males are conceived to every 100 females. By the time of birth, the ratio of males to females has dropped to about 106:100 in the United States (whites only) and in Britain, and to about 98:100 in India. The Indian figure suggests that nutrition affects the sex ratio, a suggestion which is supported by a comparison of the sex ratio at birth between different socio-economic groups within the same society. (However, nutrition is not the whole explanation: it cannot, for example, account for the difference between Aden and Monserrat, which have recorded relatively stable sex ratios at birth of 120:100 and 94:100 for the years 1949-1964.)

More males than females are miscarried or stillborn—the sex ratio of aborted foetuses falls between 120:100 and 160:100—and more males than females die of birth trauma. 54% more males than females die of birth injuries, and 18% more of congenital malformations. (The higher rate of birth injuries among males may be connected with their greater weight and head circumference.) In the first year of life 54% of all deaths are male—a ratio which stays strikingly constant. At the age of 21, male deaths make up 68% of the total; at 35 they make up 58% and at 55, 64%. Beyond 65-70 the difference

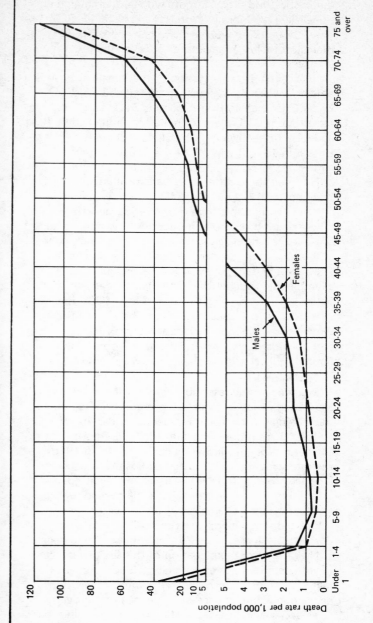

4 Mortality rates of white males and females at different ages, United States, 1950.

diminishes, and after 75 more women than men die, since there are more women than men still alive. After 85 far more women than men appear in the mortality tables, a fact that testifies to their longevity.

In fact the life expectation of the female at birth is almost universally higher than that of the male. In Britain, life expectation at birth is 74.8 years for females, but 68.1 years for males; in China it is 65.6 and 61.3 respectively; in Brazil, 45.5 and 41.8. In Britain in 1841 it was 42.2 for a female and 40.2 for a male.

How can these differences be explained? A breakdown of the mortality figures shows that men are more susceptible than women to some hazards. Where death is due to non-infectious diseases, some of the excess in male deaths is due to the preponderance in males of diseases and defects transmitted by sex-linked mutant genes. However, epilepsy, for example, has roughly the same incidence in both sexes, but the death rate from it is about 30% higher in males. Recent research suggests that one of the female sex hormones, progesterone, may be an anti-convulsive and sedative agent, so some of the female's superior survival capacity may come from her hormones.

Women are also less liable to die from accidents in the home, which in most Western countries are now the leading cause of death in people under 45. In almost all age groups, mortality from domestic accidents is greater in the male. In the UK in 1960 the ratio was about 2:1 in age groups 0-4 and 15-44 (the age group 5-14 is not so unevenly balanced, and after 65 more females than males die because of the greater number of females alive.) One expert has calculated that generally the male risk of death in domestic accidents is 2 to 5 times that of the female.

No satisfactory explanation of this sex difference in vulnerability has yet been given. The argument that males and females lead different kinds of lives, and hence one would expect a difference in their death rates, lacks evidence. Domestic accidents, for instance should, according to this line of reasoning, kill more females than males, since females spend more of their lives at home. Another theory which has been put forward to account for the male infant's greater vulnerability suggests that males may explore the environment more actively than females, thus increasing their risks of accident and death. This is an interesting speculation but it is strictly unproven. In fact the female seems to have a superior capacity for survival which does not come from living a different kind of life.

Confirmation of this comes from a recent study of women smokers prepared by the American Cancer Society. Although the common belief is that more men than women die from the effects of tobacco smoking because men smoke more heavily than women, this study shows that there is actually a sex difference in resistance to the effects of tobacco on health: females are constitutionally more resistant. A group of heavy women smokers was compared with a group of heavy men smokers, and the female risk of disease and mortality was found to be substantially lower than the male risk. The females' risk of heart artery disease and lung cancer was about half that of the male group.

For a third category of deaths, those due to the infectious diseases, the figures again show an impressive tendency to favour the female. In the first year of life, 23% more males than females die of diarrhoea and enteritis, 22% more of influenza and pneumonia. In the first three weeks of life, more than twice as many males die from infectious diseases. Per million population of all ages, infectious diseases killed 102 males but only 60 females in England and Wales in 1969.

This male susceptibility to infectious diseases, and to mortality from them, has been directly connected with the difference in chromosomal make-up between male and female. Genes controlling the mechanisms by which the body withstands infection are transmitted via the X chromosome. This means that mutant genes responsible for failures in the body's resistance to infection are also transmitted on the X chromosome. As with such diseases as haemophilia, the female's inheritance of two X chromosomes from two parents makes the dominance of a mutant gene impossible unless the other X chromosome suffers from the same weakness, which is extremely unlikely to happen. But the male who receives an X chromosome from his mother with a mutant gene attached will suffer from the effects of this gene, since there is no other healthy X chromosome to balance it. The hypothesis that resistance to infection is, in part at least, a function under the control of genes is well supported by the evidence. The male's higher susceptibility has a distinct biochemical basis.

A fourth category of death, suicide, also shows a sex difference. Stengel's classic study 'Suicide and Attempted Suicide' shows that the majority of suicides in most countries for which we have figures are male. In England and Wales in 1961 three males killed themselves for every two females. But the probable significance of the sex difference in the suicide rate is easily inflated. It is important to note that whilst males outnumber females in successful suicides, the reverse is true of attempted suicides. Accurate figures for the latter are hard to come by, but the ratio is probably about one male suicide attempt for every two or three female suicide attempts. A study of psychological disturbance in adolescence revealed a sex ratio in suicide attempts of 3.5 females to 1 male, and in actual suicides of 3.4 males to 1 female—an exact and puzzling reversal.

The sex difference in the incidence of suicide is correlated with characteristically male and female methods. Of 1,000 males who committed suicide between 1955 and 1959 in the United States, over half used firearms and explosives, whereas a quarter of a comparable 1,000 female suicides did so. Second in popularity among males was hanging and strangulation, which came third among females. The dominant method used by females (346 out of 1,000) was poisoning and asphyxiation. The sex difference in the method used is also one of lethality; in the male's

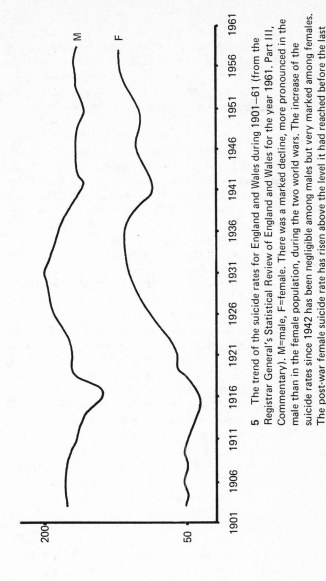

5   The trend of the suicide rates for England and Wales during 1901–61 (from the Registrar General's Statistical Review of England and Wales for the year 1961. Part III, Commentary). M=male, F=female. There was a marked decline, more pronounced in the male than in the female population, during the two world wars. The increase of the suicide rates since 1942 has been negligible among males but very marked among females. The post-war female suicide rate has risen above the level it had reached before the last war, while the male rate has remained well below it.

methods the 'point of no return' is reached far sooner. Thus, there may be many failed suicides among females that are due to the unreliability of poisoning and asphyxiation in guaranteeing death.

The choice of method may be explained either by the fact that guns, explosives, etc, are more readily available to men, or by a sex difference in the intention to succeed. Probably some of both is involved, but the fact that comparable proportions (35% and 39%) of female and male suicides, both attempted and committed, leave suicide notes, does not support the second explanation. A further point to consider is that the sex ratio is not a stable one. Most of the increase in suicide since 1949 is accounted for by female suicides. In 1952 in England and Wales 4,343 people committed suicide: in 1961, 5,216. Out of the total increase of 873, 639 were females and 234 males. (See Figure 5.)

Suicide is linked both to mental illness and to social situation, both of which are differentiated by sex. Mental illness or disorder is thought to be the main or contributory cause of suicide in about half the total number of cases. For all mental disorders as a whole, the male incidence is higher. But the results of many studies indicate that some forms of mental illness tend to be female, while others are male. Manic depressive illness seems to affect females more than males; schizophrenia, males more than females (Table 1 shows a preponderance of females, but other studies do not agree with this, and suggest that the ratio is something like 117 males to 100 females). However, these ratios vary from one society to another and even within the same society according to age, social situation and geographical location. Males also suffer more from the alcoholic psychoses in a ratio of something like 5:1 and women suffer more from the psychoneurotic disorders in ratios varying from about 2:1 to about 5:3.

The greater tendency of the male of any age to suffer from mental disorder or psychological disturbance is borne out by studies of adolescent delinquency and referrals to child guidance clinics.

diagnostic category	males	females
acute and chronic brain disorder	6.6	3.7
mental deficiency	2.2	1.7
psychotic disorders:	24.1	29.4
schizophrenia	20.8	22.8
other	3.3	6.6
psychoneurotic disorders:	20.0	31.9
anxiety reaction	8.0	10.0
depressive reaction	6.9	14.1
obsessive-compulsive reaction	1.7	1.8
other	3.4	5.1
personality disorders:	40.9	25.1
passive-aggressive personality	12.5	8.5
sociopathic personality*	4.9	1.2
schizoid personality	4.3	2.6
emotionally unstable personality	2.1	3.6
inadequate personality	3.4	2.3
other	13.7**	6.9
transient situational personality disorder	4.3	6.0

* includes antisocial reaction and sexual deviation
** includes 6.2% alcohol addiction.

TABLE 1 Diagnoses of patients in psychiatric clinics. The columns show the percentages of the adult male and female psychiatric populations suffering from each disorder. (Based on samples of 33,046 males and 49,966 females.)

The latter almost invariably show a preponderance of males in an overall ratio of roughly 2½:1. (See Table 2.) The biggest sex difference is in the frequency of referrals for 'aggressive and anti-social behaviour', where the ratio is something like 4:1. Is this because the male is constitutionally more aggressive? A clue is provided in the fact that boys are referred 2½ times as often as girls for excessively passive, withdrawn, asocial behaviour. (The same pattern of behaviour inappropriate to their sex occurs in adolescents and adults referred to psychiatric clinics.) In other words, parental expectations about sex-appropriate behaviour—relatively outward-directed and aggressive for males, relatively passive and inward-directed for females—clearly play an important role in determining the pattern of referrals for 'abnormal' behaviour. Children of either sex who do not behave in a fashion appropriate to their sex are considered to be problems. It has been suggested that social adjustment is made more difficult for boys (and referrals to clinics therefore more likely) because aggressive behaviour is not socially tolerated beyond a certain point although aggressive behaviour itself is encouraged.

The difficulties children have in fulfilling their parents' expectations of sex-appropriate roles may in themselves be psychologically disturbing. A recent research study into the background of schizophrenics has produced the suggestion that one factor may be a clash between the child's own personality and what the parents expect of him or her as 'normal' sex-role behaviour. A recurrent finding, which prompted this explanation, is that schizophrenic females are more active and 'masculine' in their behaviour and interests than normal females, and schizophrenic males more passive and 'feminine'.

To the extent that males show more deviant behaviour suggesting minor brain damage, the sex difference may be due to the physical conditions of birth. Apart from the mechanical problems of delivery which beset male infants more than female, significantly more males fail to breathe within

40

referral problems	males	females	total	total as % of N
academic difficulties	829	297	1,126	45
mental retardation	412	261	673	27
aggressive and anti-social behaviour	594	161	755	30
passive, withdrawn, asocial behaviour	382	164	546	22
emotional instability and anxiety symptoms	407	173	580	23
hyperactivity and motor symptoms	252	100	352	14
sexual behaviour problems	37	23	60	2.5
toilet training	113	48	161	6.5
speech defects	123	38	161	6.5
miscellaneous	209	135	344	14

TABLE 2 Distribution of 'referral problems' in four child guidance centres. The total number of children involved (N) was 2,500 and there was an average of 1.9 complaints per child.

two-and-a-half minutes of birth, a condition which is known to be associated with brain damage, often not serious enough to need treatment.

If one looks at the whole field of deviant behaviour (including suicide and mental disorder, and also criminality, which is dealt with in Chapter 2) one finds that in every area of deviancy there are far fewer females than males. Is this because of some biological/psychological difference between the sexes, or is it a direct consequence of the difference in life-pattern and social situation? The nature-nurture debate has raged particularly fiercely here.

Proponents of 'nature' as the origin of the male's greater deviancy point to the differences in aggression between the sexes as a factor responsible for criminal, suicidal and anti-social tendencies. To some extent, aggression *is* biologically determined. A study of 1,250 prisoners guilty of crimes of violence has correlated their record for asocial aggression with the 'brain waves' recorded on an electroencephalograph (EEGs). A distinction emerged between 'habitual aggressors' and those who had committed a single violent crime (usually with provocation). The latter group had EEGs within the range of normality, but 57% of the former group had abnormal EEGs. The site of EEG abnormality in these habitual aggressors was the same as in a form of (temporal-lobe) epilepsy which is thought to be due to a congenital fault in the early maturation of the brain. This fact, together with the greater vulnerability of the male foetus to death and deformity, may help to account for some of the asocial aggressiveness of the male, and so may contribute to the imbalance in the sex ratio for certain types of violent crime. A link between the Y chromosome and criminal behaviour has been suggested, due to the finding that criminal populations appear to have a high incidence of the XYY chromosome constitution. However, the incidence of this abnormality in the general male population is now known to be high (something like 1 in 350) and it is thought to be the most common chromosome abnormality in males; thus, there may be no more

XYY criminals than there are XYY individuals in the non-criminal population.

Among the possible biological explanations of the male's greater deviancy, the role of the sex hormones may seem a likely candidate. It is known that male hormones injected into animals make them more aggressive. When two male mice meet they usually fight while females and castrated males do not; castrated males treated with male hormones become as aggressive as normal male mice. But in humans the relationship between hormone levels and behaviour is not nearly as simple as it appears to be in some animals, and very little is really known about it.

Since the primary function of the sex hormones is to ensure adult reproductive ability, it is hardly surprising that they affect sexual behaviour. However the way in which they do so is interesting and unexpected. One might suppose that the strength of the sexual drive would depend on the presence of the appropriate hormones—the male hormone in men and the female in women. This is not so. In fact it is the male hormone that is related to the sexual drive in both men and women. The removal of a man's testes usually threatens the potency of his sexual drive; the removal of a woman's ovaries does not. Conversely, when women are given androgenic hormones in the course of medical treatment they produce a striking increase in sexual desire, even when the women are seriously ill. Thus androgen acts as an equaliser in balancing the sexual drives of male and female; it is significant that at all ages beyond puberty there is a far greater similarity in androgen production between the sexes than there is in the production of female hormones.

(The most likely source of the androgens responsible for female libido is the adrenal glands. A study of twenty-nine women who had ovaries and adrenals removed in the treatment of breast cancer showed no adverse effect on sexual drive, activity or response when only the ovaries were removed, but in the women who lost both ovaries and adrenal glands

43

the sexual drive was either lessened or abolished.)
Androgens also affect muscular strength and
energy, by influencing the metabolism of nitrogen in
the body, and they may therefore be responsible for
some of the differences in weight, strength and
energy between the sexes in some populations. Dr
John Money, in the encyclopaedic two-volume study
of 'Sex and Internal Secretions', describes the cases of
two men he treated for deficiency of testicular
hormones. After treatment with androgens, these
men, both manual labourers, noted a marked rise in
their fatigue thresholds. Two women also treated by
him, who were suffering from an excess of male
hormones secreted by the adrenal glands, noted a
parallel decline in muscular strength and energy after
the treatment had cut down their excess of androgens. How far this sort of finding is applicable to the
majority of normal males and females is not known.
Considerable attempts have been made from time
to time to correlate the hormonal differences in men
and women with facets of everyday human behaviour. One such attempt, by Dr Katherina Dalton,
relates various aspects of women's social and
emotional behaviour to the hormonal fluctuations of
the menstrual cycle. Dr Dalton claims to have shown
that schoolgirls achieve lower grades in academic
work in the week preceding menstruation, and that
women are more prone to beat their children, commit
crimes, miss work, have accidents, attempt suicides
and acquire bacterial and virus infections during
menstruation and the week or so preceding it. This is
attributed to the 'premenstrual syndrome', a
condition characterised by a constellation of
symptoms, including depression, irritability,
tiredness, breast tenderness and weight increase. The
suggested cause of this syndrome is a hormone
imbalance in which the ovary does not produce
enough progesterone. The body is then said to make
up for this by taking extra from the adrenal glands,
leaving them short of the amount needed to produce
a group of chemicals known as the cortico-steroids.
44   The shortage of these, in turn, results in water

retention (weight increase), alterations in the blood sugar level and so on.

The chief implication of this research is that hormonal factors may be directly responsible for greater emotional instability in women. However, there are various problems connected with this assertion. First, the relationship between the menstrual cycle and psychological/emotional states is not only one-way. The onset of menstruation (and thus the timing of the menstrual cycle) is known to be influenced by states of mind and emotion. Secondly, the various correlates of the premenstrual syndrome charted by Dr Dalton (including the greater likelihood of admission to a mental hospital, attempted suicide, criminal behaviour, infectious illness in the children of the 'afflicted' women and decreases in the earnings of their husbands) may not have a great deal of statistical significance. One reason is that the period preceding and following the onset of menstruation used in the analysis covers a time span of up to twelve days, and statistics are related to this rather than to the presence or absence of the physical condition known as the premenstrual syndrome. Furthermore, one would expect roughly half of any sample of women to be somewhere in this twelve-day stage of their menstrual cycle at any particular time, since the whole cycle takes between three weeks and a month; therefore a substantial number of any events or tendencies in any sample could be expected to fall within this period. (See Chapter 5 for a further comment on menstruation and behaviour.)

No one has yet demonstrated a biochemical connection between changing emotional conditions and the physiological changes accompanying the menstrual cycle. Until they do there seems to be no possible justification in treating all women as though irregularities in their behaviour were due to the constant ebb and flow of their hormones, and certainly not for propounding the theory that menstruation fits women only for particular, restricted, roles in life. The social situations of

relatively isolated motherhood and housewifery
which occur in our society may be just as great a
source of stress or anxiety as the hormonal stresses of
menstruation. In any case, one needs here to make a
comparison between the sexes. Men, too, often suffer
from considerable stresses—from their jobs for
instance—but there is also some evidence that they
are subject to cyclic emotional variations. Since
research in this field has concentrated almost
exclusively on women, we have no way of telling
what fundamental sex difference there is, if any.

Is there any basis for supposing that hormones
govern male and female behaviour in general? Recent
investigations with animals show that, in the species
studied, sex differentiation cannot be explained
solely in term of hormones. The brain also seems to be
involved. For example, female rats injected with
testosterone in the critical early period of sex
differentiation (in rats, the first four days after birth)
failed to develop as females not only with respect to
reproductive function but also in areas of related
behaviour. They lost the 'lordosis' response to males,
which consists of arching the back and rearing up the
pelvis, and developed male patterns of behaviour,
especially with regard to aggression. Correspondingly,
male rats castrated after birth became sensitive to
very small doses of female hormones, and developed
the lordosis response of normal females. (Uncastrated
males do not respond to female hormones.) With
monkeys, these findings have been duplicated.
Pregnant monkeys dosed with androgen have given
birth to females with masculinised genitalia who later
behave in a 'masculine' way to other, normal females.
They threaten, take the initiative and engage in rough
and tumble play more often than normal controls,
and they also attempt to mount the normal females
in a typically male manner. This group of masculinised females have so far shown these signs of
masculinity into the third year of life, though many
of the aggressive male characteristics diminish in
strength as time passes.

46   The explanation of these findings is that initially

the brain is not differentiated for males and females, but before or just after birth (dependent on the species) sex hormones act on it, as they do on the undifferentiated genital tract, to organise specific circuits in the brain and the central nervous system into male or female patterns. The result of this is that the sensitivity of the brain to the sex hormones is itself differentiated by sex. In the absence of testosterone, both male and female are sensitive to female hormones and capable of displaying female behaviour. Testosterone makes the brain specifically sensitive only to male hormones.

The difficulties of generalising from other species to man (and woman) are legion. David Hamburg and Donald Lunde asked in 1967:

6 If a similar relation between androgen and aggressive behaviour exists in homo sapiens, how might it express itself? In view of the enormous dependence of the human species on learning processes, it seems quite unlikely that the early exposure of hypo-thalamic [brain] cells to androgen would establish fixed, complex patterns of aggressive behaviour for a lifetime. It is much more likely that early exposure to androgen would affect humans in more subtle ways. Perhaps the influence of androgen during a critical period in brain development on the circuits destined later to mediate aggressive behaviour would have CNS [central nervous system] differentiating effects that would facilitate ease of learning aggressive patterns and increase readiness to learn such patterns...Or, certain patterns of action might become more rewarded as a result of the early hormone action on the central nervous system...The possibilities for experimental analysis of this problem in higher primates are potentially quite important for understanding the development of aggressive behaviour in man. Such an approach should take into consideration the interactions of genes, hormones and learning processes. 9

47   This is speculation, however. First, it is not clear that

sex hormones do in fact produce patterns of brain sensitivity that endure for a lifetime (the animal evidence does not indicate that they do). Second, generalisations from one species to another are not really valid. Reproductive behaviour is generally controlled by hormones and chromosomes but in some species the hormones are not part of the mechanism of control. Humans, on the other hand, impose an additional control—learning—and it is the human ability to learn which makes generalisation from other species difficult and of dubious value.

2

Sex and person- ality

Only the everyday observation of men and women in society is needed to 'prove' that differences of personality follow the biological differences of sex. Men are more aggressive and independent than women; they are braver, more outgoing and extroverted, confident in their own ability to control and manipulate the external environment. Women are more sensitive and perceptive in their relationships with other people; they are more dependent on these relationships. They are introverted and domesticated and emotionally labile.

In 1936 Lewis M Terman and Catharine Cox Miles published a book called 'Sex and Personality' which is an account of the attempt to establish scientifically the norms of masculinity and femininity—the differences in personality between the sexes—in our society. The Masculinity—Femininity Test, as they called it, is a pencil and paper test in questionnaire form, consisting of 910 items. These items are divided into a number of sections: in section I, for example, the subject is asked to choose which of a set of four words he or she associates with another word. Examples are *date* (appointment, dance, fruit, history) and *moon* (light, month, night, round). On the whole, male and female subjects differ in their responses. Male responses are 'dance', 'fruit' and 'history' for date, and 'light' for moon. Female responses are 'appointment' for date and 'night' and 'round' for moon. ('Month' is apparently neutral.)

The purpose of the test is to measure the extent to which a subject's responses diverge or accord with the average for his or her sex on those items to which the sexes respond differently. The items used are those which experience has shown do differentiate between the sexes. Questions which male and female subjects answer in the same way ('Do you like modern art?') are discarded. Resulting scores show that males and females tend to score within certain specific ranges, and that scores for each sex cluster around a different point (the sex-specific mean).

The sex differences in the average scores of male and female can be defined in detail. In word association, females tend to choose words for articles of dress, personal adornment, colours, aesthetic appraisal, domestic things and happenings, and words indicating a 'kind' and 'sympathetic' social orientation. Conversely, the male preference is for words describing outdoor phenomena, activity and adventure, science and machinery, political, business and commercial enterprises. These sex differences are underlined by the Rorschach ink blot interpretation test. Again, females pick domestic occupations, aesthetic expression and personal adornment: males, machinery, physical science and outdoor pursuits. Sections of the test which inquire into information possessed by males and females about specific items, show that the key masculine quality is 'the aggressive, adventurous, enterprising, outwardly directed disposition: the tendency to pugnacity and self-assertiveness'. The outstanding feminine traits are 'the actively sympathetic, the inwardly directed disposition: the maternal impulse and the tender feelings; concern with domestic affairs'. Other sections show females to be more tearful and easily disgusted than males, to pity the weak and the helpless, to make judgments that are more emotional and less objective than the male's, signifying an introvertive response; to be more emotionally expressive in general, to prefer 'ministrative' occupations, to prefer domestic incidents in literature, while the male chooses external adventure.

The success of Terman and Miles' Masculinity-Femininity Test in differentiating between personality types by sex confirms that everyday observations of sex differences are grounded in fact. Men and women *are* temperamentally different. But what does this 'fact' mean? It means that personality differences between male and female exist within Western society with a certain constancy and stability. But it does not mean that these differences are moulded by biology—indeed, it says nothing at all about how much of the difference is due to biology and how much to culture.

The personality differences emerging from the

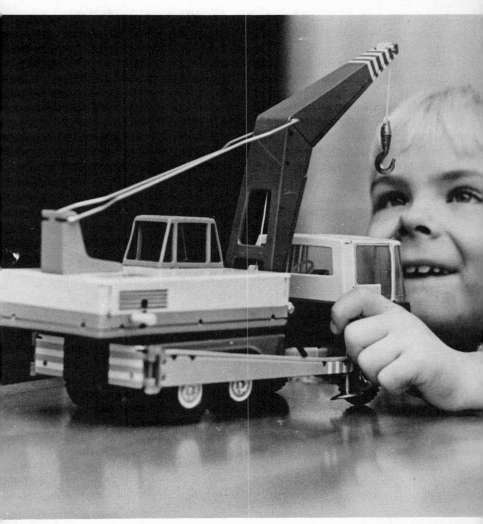

(Fotolink)

Masculinity-Femininity Test appear in children as well as adults. Not only are temperamental sex differences in evidence from childhood on, but they also exist as conscious ideals of masculinity and femininity by which behaviour is judged. Five-year-olds view the male as more competent, more aggressive, more fear-arousing and less nurturant than the female, and they adjust their own behaviour accordingly. Preferences in toys often neatly reflect the awareness children have of sex-appropriate behaviour. The list in Table 3 was found in one study to differentiate consistently and markedly between boys and girls: the boys' choices are for toys symbolising physical and mechanical activity and the world outside the home, those of girls for toys of the domestic interior, reflecting domesticity, nurturance, and aesthetic adornment.

The finding that sex differences in personality can be traced back to childhood suggests that, if they are not moulded in biology, then they must emerge very early in the process of cultural learning. The increase that occurs with age in sex differentiation (of personality types, preferences in toys etc) points to a strong cultural influence—as also does the fact that people are aware of the opposition between masculinity and femininity and the need to conform to one ideal or other in socially visible ways. Terman and Miles, in their early use of the Masculinity-Femininity Test, noted the marked correlation of masculine-feminine scores with certain social-cultural factors, including age, education, measured IQ and social class. Length of education, for instance, is correlated with greater femininity for males and greater masculinity for females. This kind of association again suggests that there is a strong component of social learning in the acquisition of masculinity and femininity.

But to distinguish more clearly between the biological and cultural causes of sex differences, we must look beyond our own society. How do other cultures define personality differences by sex? Do they make a

toy	rating
wheelbarrow	3.2
cleaning set	8.4
plane	1.7
sports car	3.6
teddy bear	5.8
rocking horse	4.6
skipping rope	7.0
blackboard	5.3
dish cabinet	8.3
football	1.5
construction set	2.7
tool set	2.0
sewing machine	8.2
dumpertruck	2.5
banjo	4.5
cosmetics	8.8
doll's pram	8.5
telephone	5.6
racing car	2.2
alphabet ball	4.9
roller skates	5.3
paddling pool	5.0
tractor	3.0
doll wardrobe	8.7

TABLE 3 Sex preferences in toys. The ratings run from 1 (strongly masculine) through 5 (appropriate for both sexes) to 9 (strongly feminine). These ratings were made by a group of twenty-year-old psychology students and proved in practice to be highly predictive of the choices made by children of each sex.

distinction between male and female, and if so do they make the same distinctions as Western culture does?

Some years ago, Margaret Mead set out specifically to study the variation in masculine and feminine personality types in different cultures. She has been accused by some of finding precisely what she set out to look for; on the other hand, the findings of other anthropologists have for a long time supported her conclusion that different societies define masculinity and femininity differently, emphasising different qualities, interests and occupations as 'male' and 'female'.

In 'Sex and Temperament in Three Primitive Societies' Margaret Mead describes three New Guinea tribes: the Arapesh, the Mundugumor and the Tchambuli. Amongst the Arapesh, the ideal adult has a gentle, passive, cherishing nature, and resembles the feminine type in our culture. In the relationships between the sexes, including the overtly sexual, the Arapesh recognise no temperamental difference at all. Neither is the initiator or the aggressor. The main 'work' of both adult men and women is child-bearing and child-rearing—indeed they call sexual intercourse 'work' when the object is conception. In the early months of pregnancy, intercourse is a duty, since the mixture of paternal semen and maternal blood is believed to form the child. The verb 'to bear a child' is used indiscriminately of both sexes. Mead observed that if one comments on a middle-aged man as good-looking, the people answer 'Good-looking? Yes. But you should have seen him before he bore all those children!'

This accentuation of parenthood and of 'femininity' in the personalities and roles of both sexes is reversed among the Mundugumor, where both sexes approximate to the masculine pattern. The women are as assertive and vigorous as the men: they detest bearing and rearing children and men in turn detest pregnancy in their wives. Both sexes are reared to be independent and hostile, and boys and girls have very similar personalities.

54   The third tribe, the Tchambuli, did show a

differentiation of personality by sex. The males approximated to our stereotype of femininity, and the females to our masculinity. In 'Male and Female' Mead reports the women to be self-assertive, practical and managing, whereas adult males 'are skittish, wary of each other, interested in art, in the theatre, in a thousand petty bits of insult and gossip. Hurt feelings are rampant...the pettishness of those who feel themselves weak and isolated. The men wear lovely ornaments [the women shave their heads and are unadorned] they do the shopping, they carve and paint and dance.'

Mead comments that 'this is the only society in which I have worked where little girls of ten and eleven were more alertly intelligent and more enterprising than little boys...the minds of small males, teased, pampered, neglected, and isolated, had a fitful, fleeting quality, an inability to come to grips with anything.'

These various cultural definitions of male and female temperament are associated with different definitions of masculine and feminine tasks. For example, a number of societies reverse our practice and give 'heavy' work to the women. Among the people of Bamenda, studied by Phyllis Kaberry, the women do all the agricultural work. They carry the heavy loads and this is said to be because they have stronger foreheads than the men. (A similar situation was found by Mead among the Arapesh, who gave the same reason for it.) Kaberry heard a group of men discussing a wifeless neighbour: 'He works hard, indeed he works almost as hard as a woman!'

Jules Henry, describing the life of a tribe in the Brazilian highlands, says of them: 'A complete lack of emphasis on temperamental differences between the sexes permits to boys and girls, men and women, the same jocular and often robust sexual aggressiveness. The term for intercourse may have either a masculine or a feminine object.' Henry points out that 'The vulgar English terms can take only feminine objects, and thus we reveal in the very grammatical form of our vulgarisms the feeling that the male is the active

55

This New Guinea girl may be carrying half a hundredweight or more, slung from her forehead in the traditional feminine way. (Anthony Forge)

and aggressive partner.'

Both men and women in this Brazilian tribe make 'open, ribald and aggressive onslaughts', including some by women on this male anthropologist himself, who professed to a belief that many of the women were stronger than men in his own country. He summarises both masculine and feminine personality in this tribe as 'practical' and 'aggressive'. A similar aggressiveness on the part of the female exists among the Zuni Indians; Ethel Albert, in a fascinating article on the roles of women in different cultures, reports that among these people the alliance of sexual aggressiveness with femininity means that the male, and not the female, faces the wedding night with fear and trembling.

Differing stereotypes of masculine and feminine temperament are often found in other societies, without there being a wholesale reversal of our own cultural patterns. Edward T Hall in his book on Iran, 'The Silent Language', describes a thoroughly patriarchal society, where women are nevertheless expected to be the practical, cool and calculating sex. Men are the ones who show emotion, being sensitive and intuitive, and preferring poetry to logic.

There would be pronounced cross-cultural disagreement on the preference for domestic occupations found by Terman and Miles in their Masculinity and Femininity Test. One instance would be women in a wide area of Africa, for, as one ethnographer put it, 'the typical woman thinks of herself as a cultivator and trader, as well as a wife and mother.' Traditionally, the role of cultivating the land and marketing its produce has been a female one. Women have developed an ability and an interest in moving freely outside the home. They have also played a very strong political role. An index of this was the Ibo revolt in 1929 when ten thousand women demonstrated against the imposition of direct taxation, and military forces had to be called in to quell the revolt. It seems that the administration of the time had vastly underestimated the independence and personal amibition of these African women, whose 'masculinised' personalities bore witness to a long tradition of female self-definition and extra-domestic activity in that part of the world.

Terman and Miles comment on the feminine proclivity for personal adornment, and on the way this is reflected in the female's choice of word associations indicating aesthetic appeal. In a number of cultures this difference between male and female personalities is reversed. Thus William Davenport writes of a Southwest Pacific society, in which

❛ Only men wear flowers in their hair and scented leaves tucked into their belts or arm bands. At formal dances it is the man who dresses in the most elegant finery and...when these young men are fully made up and costumed for the dance they are considered so irresistible to women that they are not allowed to be alone, even for a moment, for fear some woman will seduce them. ❜

And even in a society where the Western sex difference in adornment is not reversed, one may find men valued for attributes Western society would consider more feminine than masculine. Thus girls in the pastoral tribe of the Bororo (in tropical Africa) choose men at dances for their 'gracefulness and beauty'.

Quite often one finds these examples of masculinity and femininity in other societies dismissed as eccentric, deviant, peculiar, and irrelevant to the mainstream of human development. This is an absurdly ethnocentric view. The history of Western culture itself contains within it precisely the same kind of reversal of today's accepted patterns. Women in Anglo-Saxon times were self-assertive and independent, like many women in Africa today, and most writers on the social history of the Middle Ages call attention to the 'masculine character' of women at that time. Anne Anastasi quotes a passage from Garreau on France in the time of the crusades:

❛ A trait peculiar to this epoch is the close resemblance

between the manners of men and women. The rule that such and such feelings or acts are permitted in one sex and forbidden to the other was not fairly settled. Men had the right to dissolve in tears, and women that of talking without prudery...If we look at their intellectual level, the women appear distinctly superior. They are more serious: more subtle. With them we do not seem to be dealing with the rude state of civilisation that their husbands belong to...As a rule, women seem to have the habit of weighing their acts; of not yielding to momentary impressions. **)**

Many anthropologists have been impressed by the degree of coherence there is in any society between adult personality and the techniques used in the early care and control of the individual. This relationship between personality and society has been extensively studied. Does it tell us anything about the origins of sex differences in personality?

One detailed study of child-rearing investigated the differences and similarities between six cultures, ranging from Kenya to Mexico and from the Phillipines to New England. In this study twenty-four children, aged from three to ten, were picked from each of the six cultures and studied by trained fieldworkers. The results indicated that boys are more likely than girls to engage in physical aggression in all six cultures, while girls have a greater tendency to act affectionately and responsibly. These sex differences were associated with differential child-rearing practices. Where boys and girls differed in the display (and kind) of aggressive behaviour, for instance, parents were usually distinguishing between them in their expectations about aggression and in their handling of it (punishment or reward). For example, mothers in the Kenyan community do little to stop fights between girls—they say that girls are less likely to hurt each other than boys (girls are weaker); but they strongly discourage fights between boys and still more so fights between boys and girls (they assume the boys are sexually motivated and cane them).

59

In this community, the greater aggression of the boys contrasts with the greater sociability (defined as making friendly approaches to others) and succourance (asking others for help) of the girls. However, among the Mexican children, boys are significantly more sociable and dependent than girls. It is notable that these Mexican parents treat boys and girls very similarly in all respects during early childhood: in later childhood (from three to six) parents continue to use physical punishment to control the girls but not the boys. The community as a whole is distinctly non-aggressive, which perhaps goes with the low achievement and self-reliance in this sample of children compared with the other samples.

Another cross-cultural survey, by Barry, Bacon and Child, this time of 110 societies but based only on the ethnographic literature, found considerable differences in the socialisation of male and female children. In particular, it found that in most of these societies there is a specific mention of social practices designed to make boys self-reliant and to encourage male achievement, while girls are trained to be nurturant, responsible and obedient. (See Table 4.)

In accounting for this consistency, the authors say that the degree to which the socialisation of the sexes differs is associated with different types of economy. They point to the association of large sex differences in child-rearing with the existence of an economy dependent upon the superior strength of the male (hunting, grain crops rather than root crops, a nomadic rather than sedentary life). Their conclusion is that these child-rearing practices are a means of ensuring the differences between male and female temperament and personality which have a practical function in such an economy. This explanation, however, has several flaws in it. Communities are found with economies requiring the exercise of strength but with very little sex differentiation of personality and role—for example, the pygmies of the Congo. (See Chapter 5.)

60

	boys	neither	girls
nurturance (33)	0	18	82
responsibility (84)	11	28	61
obedience (69)	3	62	35
achievement (31)	87	10	3
self-reliance (82)	85	15	0

TABLE 4 Differences between cultures in encouraging certain qualities in boys and girls. The columns show, for each quality, the percentage of cultures in which there was evidence of greater encouragement for boys, girls or neither. (The figures in brackets are the number of cultures for which there was rateable information.)

Nevertheless, there is a well-established correlation between sex differentials in child-rearing practices and distinguishable male and female personality types. In 'Patterns of Child Rearing' Sears, Maccoby and Levin discuss the sex differences in parental treatment of children which were clearly evident in their sample of 379 five-year-olds. The area in which they found the greatest and most consistent differences was that of aggression, both in the children's behaviour and in parental expectations and treatment of aggression. Boys were allowed more aggression in their relationships with other children; aggression in girls was discouraged. Aggression towards parents was treated very non-permissively if it came from girls, but boys were allowed more freedom of expression. For some mothers, being 'boylike' meant being aggressive. Boys were often encouraged to fight back if another child started a fight: girls were not. The authors comment that, whatever the evidence for biological factors in aggression, the mothers in their sample did not rely on the impact of biology to create masculine -aggressive boys and feminine-non-aggressive girls. The mothers' own reaction to biological maleness and femaleness in terms of sex-differentiated expectation, reward and punishment, made up a learning experience for the child, the influence of which it is difficult to discount.

Aggression has become one of the main qualities used in defining and comparing masculine and feminine behaviour. L A Hattwick (in 1937) observed a large sample of nursery school children aged from two to four and a half, and concluded that the most outstanding sex difference in behaviour was the prevalence in males of aggressive approaches to other children, negativism towards adults, marked physical activity and 'non-social behaviour problems of the overt type' (wriggling, refusing to sleep at rest time, handling the genitals). The report was one of the first in a long line, which cumulatively highlight the probability that these sex differences in aggressiveness either begin at birth or are generated at some very early point in children's lives. The mass of observational data contained in these reports ranges from the simple timing and description of aggressive incidents in the behaviour of boys and girls to studies of the fantasy role of aggression in dollplay. The former show that males exceed females not only in amount of aggressive activity but in the degree to which they initiate it and in the display of aggression as a response to frustration, a reaction which is relatively weak in girls. It is also evident that at an early age aggression is valued in boys by other boys, whereas in female peer-group culture it is not.

Unfortunately the observational studies do not cover the first two years of life, a period when cultural conditioning may take its toll of spontaneity in both males and females. Attempts have been made to relate sex differences in the behaviour of newborn infants with the differences observed in childhood and beyond, but though the results are suggestive they are not conclusive, because of the small samples involved and the difficulties of interpreting the relatively undifferentiated behaviour of the infant. Schaffer and Emerson, in a study undertaken in 1964, concluded that although some infants seemed to avoid or dislike being held, carried, stroked and kissed, this was not due to any characteristic of the mother's behaviour but rather to the infant's own restlessness and dislike of restraint. More of these infants were male than female, though the difference was not statistically significant. Elsewhere there are reports of sex differences in the way some newborn infants avoid close physical contact; among the findings are a greater restlessness in boy babies before feeding (girls are restless afterwards) and a tendency on the part of boys to fall asleep readily after being fed.

From childhood to adult life there is a significant relationship between aggression (or physical assertiveness) and body size. Some studies have found a relationship between muscle mass and behaviour— the more muscular children tend in some cases to be more aggressively active: another found that the most aggressive adolescent boys are generally the larger, while girls show differences in aggression which in some instances correlate with body size. Is this because mothers view the muscular child as more dominant and assertive, or because body size is biologically related in some way to the display of aggression? The fact that girls exceeding the norm for their sex in size and muscularity also exceed the female norm for aggressive behaviour would support both these hypotheses.

Aggression has become a key word in the literature on sex differences and is used to cover a considerable range of behaviours and temperamental traits. Osgood has shown that adults tend to think of aggressive behaviour as very closely related to potency and activity, whereas passive-dependent behaviour is associated with impotence and inactivity. The same association is evident in the behavioural and temperamental differences between male and female in our society. At early ages there is a trend towards greater dependency on the part of girls, and at older ages girls rate consistently higher on measures of dependency, and lower on measures of physical assertiveness. One of the most interesting findings on aggression and dependency emerged from research conducted by Jerome Kagen and Howard Moss at the Fels Research Institute in America. They took a sample of 45 female and 44 male subjects and studied them from birth through to early adulthood—a very valuable opportunity to examine the relationship between childhood and adult behaviour. Across this time span, Kagan and Moss found that the greatest consistency occurs for males in the area of aggression, whereas for females it is in the area of passivity. A male's adult aggressiveness is predictable from his record of aggression in childhood, but his passivity in adulthood is not related to the degree of passivity he exhibited as a child. Similarly, one cannot predict the adult female's aggressiveness from childhood observation of her behaviour, but one can predict her degree of passivity. One interpretation of this finding might reasonably be that the biological drives responsible for this sex difference account for the remarkable consistency in female-passive and male-aggressive behaviour. But Kagan and Moss show conclusively that the change in the female's aggressiveness and the male's passivity is associated with, and therefore probably caused by, specific social factors.

Like Sears, Maccoby and Levin, they report distinct sex differences in parental treatment of both aggression and passivity. Passivity in boys is frowned upon and discouraged, as is aggressiveness in girls. Although there is no significant sex difference in passivity-dependency before school age, after children begin school (and presumably come under the influence of their peer-groups and teachers) male dependency and passivity show a marked drop and are replaced by a more active and retaliatory attitude. Sex differences in aggression which are visible in preschool years become more pronounced after school entry, and the girls in the sample who, in their first six years, were likely to attack other children physically, were least likely to be retaliatory as adults. Excessive aggressiveness in a school-age girl is brought under control by patterns of rewards and punishments emanating from parent, teacher and peer, and it is also probably diluted by the greater identification with females (that is, non-aggressive models) that has been shown to occur in girls during later childhood.

The differences between boys and girls in aggression are not absolute. Girls use verbal aggression more than boys: boys use physical aggression more than girls. Girls show more 'prosocial' aggression— that is, they are fond of stating rules together with threats of punishment for breaking them. The difference in aggression between the sexes is a latent rather than a manifest one. This is shown by the finding that females in general display more guilt and conflict over aggression than do males. In confronting aggression, either in their own behaviour or in somebody else's, they are less able to accept and recognise it, and this inability is accompanied by feelings of guilt, conflict and anxiety. The suggested reason for this is the inhibition of aggression the female child receives as part of her sex-role training, an inhibition which is probably strengthened by the feelings adults have about the importance of both sexes behaving in ways that accord with their roles.

Sex differences in aggression have been used in turn to explain sex differences in other fields, particularly in the statistics of suicide, homicide and criminal behaviour. Suicide and homicide are forms of aggressive behaviour: in the first the aggression is self-directed while in the second it is other-directed, and it is claimed that both propensities occur more readily in the male. As for the crime rates, these certainly show a distinct differentiation by sex which may be due to a number of factors: those that stand out are the social factors—the links between criminal behaviour and social situation, between the type of crime and social expections of masculine or feminine behaviour.

The overall incidence of criminal convictions shows a ratio of around 7 or 8 males to every female. The crimes committed tend to be differentiated by sex, and so also do the ages of the offenders. The female offender is likely to have committed a property offence, and unlikely to have been responsible for a sexual offence or a crime of violence (0.4% of all sexual offences were committed by females in England and Wales in 1965, and 5.1% of all indictable offences of violence). The female offender tends to be older than her male counterpart (21.6% of male crimes are committed by people aged 17-21, but only 13.9% of female crimes; but twice as many female crimes as male crimes are committed by people aged 40-50).

Thus the different patterns of male and female criminal behaviour appear to reflect the male's greater aggressiveness and greater tendency to deviance. But the crimes themselves reflect the different social and personal circumstances of male and female offenders, and it is only by looking at some of the ways in which crime figures are arrived at that we can see the

crime	number of males	number of females
larceny from shops	17,775	17,936
larceny from person	752	102
theft of motor cars	2,081	14
theft from unattended vehicles	10,736	166
frauds, deceit and forgery	6,390	1,529
malicious damage	1,137	44
robbery	1,412	65
burglary and housebreaking	11,412	506
sex offences	5,271	20

TABLE 5 Male and female offenders in certain categories of crime. (The figures are for England and Wales in 1965.)

connections between criminal behaviour and sex-typed social roles.

It is likely, for example, that the relatively low number of female offenders is partly due to the fact that the courts are more lenient towards females—particularly young females. Several authorities suggest that there may be far more delinquency and youthful crime among females than there appears to be. One study of undetected delinquent behaviour revealed that the crimes committed, but concealed, by girls (and therefore remaining undetected) tend to be 'male' crimes—property destruction, unauthorised driving away, and 'gang fighting'. Hence one might reasonably conclude that the patterns of male and female crime are tied to cultural patterns of masculinity and femininity, so that the type and the amount of crime committed by each sex express both sex-typed personality and sex-typed social role. Male and female gravitate towards different varieties of crime. Also, the legal treatment of male and female offenders reflects conceptions of masculinity and femininity (so that courts are, for example, more ready to believe that a girl was 'led' into crime by a boy, than vice versa) and where deviations from sex-typed criminal behaviour occur, there are more often successful attempts to conceal them.

Moreover, the law does not treat male and female alike, so that it would indeed be surprising to find an equality of the sexes in criminal statistics. For example, the category of 'sexual offences', in which there are more crimes by men, includes homosexual offences: since homosexuality is in many countries illegal only for men, women clearly cannot be convicted of this 'crime'. In Table 5, males are shown to have committed 5,271 sex offences, and 1,478 of these were homosexual. This sex difference in criminality is a consequence of legal definition; and though male homosexuality may exceed female homosexuality for other reasons (see Chapters 4 and 6) its role as a criminal statistic is a legal construct.

'Rape' is similarly defined as an exclusively male offence. There is no legal provision for a situation in which the woman is the aggressor and the man the victim, and it is not recognised by the law that a woman can initiate intercourse. Such purely legal definitions of the range of sexual behaviour possible for men and women are bound to affect the picture of their actual behaviour conveyed by the crime statistics.

An illustration of this is provided by a study of forcible rape. Menachem Amir, taking a sample of 626 rape victims and 1,292 offenders, found that in nearly 90% of the cases only 'temptation' and 'verbal coercion' were used—there was no physical violence. In other words, the female was simply 'persuaded' to have intercourse. Moreover, one fifth of the victims had a police record, usually for sexual misconduct. In one third of the cases alcohol had been drunk, and about two thirds of the times when this happened both victim and offender had been drinking. These findings hardly support the conventional stereotype of the rapist as a physically violent, aggressive and perverted male, taking his pleasure from a chaste and innocent female. Rather, they show that the definition of 'rape' is strictly external to the actual event, which is more likely to take place in the context of a social relationship between male and female than it is to represent a physically aggressive coercion on the part of the male. These legal definitions accord with the conventional types of masculine and feminine personality in our culture, and so inevitably distort the criminal statistics in a similar, sex-differentiated way.

Menachem Amir also wrote: 'Violent behaviour appears more dependent on cultural differences than on sex differences, traditionally considered of paramount importance in the expression of aggression.' He bases this statement partly on a study (in Philadelphia) of 588 homicides. In this study white males had a rate of 3.4 homicides per 100,000 population, whereas the rate for non-white males was 92 per 100,000. Within each group (white and non-white) the female rate was lower, but the non-white female rate was between 2 and 4 times higher than that of the white male.

Attention to differences between the sexes in patterns of crime inevitably obscures the similarities. In some countries, and some categories of crime, the sex difference has narrowed considerably in recent years, suggesting that, as some of the differences between the sex roles are reduced by the conditions of modern life, the deviance of male and female becomes more alike. For both male and female, the most common offence is against property, and property offences now constitute the largest single category of crime.

A comparative examination of male and female property offences reveals some interesting facts, and many of these suggest that criminal behaviour is strongly correlated with social situation, which of course is differentiated by sex.

Since the 1840s shoplifting has been considered as the most typically and specifically female type of crime. A 1962 study by T C N Gibbens and J Prince investigated 882 female and 452 male shoplifters. They found that male and female shoplifters characteristically stole different items of different value on different days of the week from different sorts of shops—that on nearly every aspect of shoplifting there was a sex difference.

Most of the things stolen were of low-value: 74% were worth under £5 and 89% under £10. The typical shoplifter in this study is female and is arrested for stealing a cheap item of clothing: she is also aged over forty, is less likely than other women of her age to be living with husband and children, and more likely to have inadequate housekeeping money (defined here as less than £5 a week in 1959). She is probably middle-class, and there is a significant chance she will be suffering from some form of mental or physical illness. She is *not* likely to be suffering from the premenstrual syndrome, which Dr Dalton has suggested is an important influence on female deviant behaviour of certain kinds (see Chapter 1).

What do these findings suggest about the reasons why female criminals are more likely to be convicted for shoplifting than for any other crime? Primarily, they suggest that, among the deviant ways in which women can respond to stress, shoplifting is the one which is both socially accepted and related to their social role. It is related to their social role because in Western society most of the buying of clothes and food is done by women in their role of housewife. (Among male shoplifters, 50% steal books.) Younger shoplifters tend to steal clothes and cosmetics, and Mark Abrams has calculated that females aged fifteen to twenty-four are responsible for nearly 40% of the total national expenditure on these things, though they only make up 13% of the population over fifteen. Obviously, the more one takes part in some form of activity the more likely one is to be guilty of deviant behaviour within it: this is true of shoplifting for females, and it is also true of many activities which are predominately male and give rise to male criminal behaviour. For instance, the incidence of car thefts is much greater for men than for women, a fact which mirrors the greater incidence of car driving among men, and the male's more developed mechanical abilities. It also reflects the fact that men spend more time outside the home than women do, a sex difference in overall activity which underlies male and female crime generally.

Otto Pollak, in his book 'The Criminality of Women', considered that the most important factor accounting for the sex difference in crime was one of social role. He believed that this accounts for the difference in the types of crimes committed by male and female, as well as for the apparent difference in incidence:

❛ The division of labour in our society assigns to women the roles of the homemaker, and rearer of children, the nurse of the sick, the domestic helper, and the passive partner in emotional relationships. It furnishes them thereby many opportunities to commit crimes in ways and by means which are not available to men, and which reduce the public character of many offences. ❜

Whatever the incidence of undetected female crime, the deviant behaviour of men and women is clearly linked to the roles and qualities of personality expected of each sex. Stealing by adolescent girls has been described as 'role-supportive' (because they steal items of personal adornment which make them attractive to males) while stealing by males has been called 'role-expressive' (because stealing is an expression of masculinity among adolescent boys). These differences in behaviour are hardly surprising in view of the differences in personality between the sexes; and since both behaviour and personality, in these instances, are correlated with social role, the sex difference appears convincingly to be more one of culture than of biology.

What is true of shoplifting is also true of some sexual deviance among females. It is related to socially sanctioned and socially expected sexual roles, and provides yet another instance in which the connection between 'sex differences' and culture is evident, while the biological explanation—if there is one—is conspicuous for its absence.

Criminality and masculinity are linked because the sort of acts associated with each have much in common. The demonstration of physical strength, a certain kind of aggressiveness, visible and external 'proof' of achievement, whether legal or illegal—these are facets of the ideal male personality and also of much criminal behaviour. Both male and criminal are valued by their peers for these qualities. Thus, the dividing line between what is masculine and what is criminal may at times be a thin one; as Albert Cohen observes in 'Delinquent Boys: the Culture of the Gang', delinquent and criminal behaviour may act as an important confirmation of masculinity.

Most of the offences committed by adolescent and adult males relate to this 'culture of the gang', a subculture in which many of the norms of middle-class society (respect for property, the need to control aggression) are turned upside down, but in which, nevertheless, the essential components of masculinity have a central place. The delinquent is therefore the 'rogue male':

❛ ...people do not simply want to excel; they want to
excel *as a man* or *as a woman,* that is to say, in those
respects, which, in their culture, are symbolic of their
respective sex roles. Furthermore, in seeking solutions
to their problems of adjustment, they seek solutions
that will not endanger their identification as
essentially male or female. Even when they adopt
behaviour which is considered disreputable by
conventional standards, the tendency is to be
disreputable in ways that are characteristically
masculine and feminine...It follows from all this that
the problems of adjustment of men and women, of
boys and girls, arise out of quite different circumstances and press for quite different solutions...both
the respectable middle class pattern and the
delinquent response are characteristically *masculine.*
Although they differ dramatically, to be sure, they
have something in common. This common element is
suggested by the words 'achievement', 'exploit',
'aggressiveness', 'daring', 'active mastery', 'pursuit'...
The delinquent response, however it may be
condemned by others on moral grounds, has at least
one virtue; it incontestably confirms, in the eyes of
all concerned, [the male's] essential masculinity. ❜

Be masculine: don't be criminal. If some men faced
with these demands feel themselves caught in a
double bind (that is, a situation in which the same
response is both demanded and punished) then
women may be caught too. Helen Hacker has
examined the theory that traditional female
personality owes a great deal to women's status as a
minority group—not 'minority' in the statistical sense,
but in the sense that women are denied privileges and
freedoms which society normally allows only to the
dominant (male) group. A comparison of women
with other minority groups, including negroes and
Jews, reveals that they show many of the psychological characteristics of minority groups. These
include a denigration of oneself or other members of

1 HIGH SOCIAL VISIBILITY

a skin colour, other 'racial'
   characteristics
b (sometimes) distinctive dress—
   bandana, flashy clothes

a secondary sex characteristics

b distinctive dress, skirts etc

2 ASCRIBED/ATTRIBUTED

a inferior intelligence, smaller
   brain, less convoluted, scarcity
   of geniuses
b more free in instinctual
   gratifications: more emotional,
   'primitive' and childlike.
   imagined sexual prowess envied
c common stereotype 'inferior'

a the same

b irresponsible, inconsistent,
   emotionally unstable
   lack strong superego
   women as 'temptresses'
c 'weaker'

3 RATIONALISATIONS OF STATUS

a thought all right in his place
b myth of contented negro

a woman's place is in the home
b myth of contented woman—
   'feminine' woman is happy in
   subordinate role

4 ACCOMMODATION ATTITUDES

a supplicatory whining intonation
   of voice
b deferential manner
c concealment of real feelings
d outwit 'white folks'
e careful study of points at
   which dominant group is
   susceptible to influence
f fake appeals for directives;
   show of ignorance

a rising inflection, smiles, laughs,
   downward glances
b flattering manner
c 'feminine wiles'
d outwit 'menfolk'
e the same

f appearance of helplessness

TABLE 6 Castelike status of women and negroes (right and left columns respectively).

the group ('I'm only a woman' 'I'm only a housewife') and hatred of other members of the group amounting to self-castigation (the 'bitchiness' of women directed at other women.) Women tend to be possibly even more prejudiced than men about the potentiality they have as a sex for full and equal participation in social, economic and political life. Helen Hacker compared the status of women and negroes, and its influence on their personalities (see Table 6).

The double bind inherent in this situation consists in the clash between the consequences of women's status as a minority group and the democratic egalitarian ideology of our society which, superficially at least, encourages women to achieve as much as men and to be equal with them at significant points in their lives—particularly during formal education. Women are thus being given two contrary directions at the same time—'Be equal' (be 'masculine') and 'Be unequal, because you are'. Anyone watching the progress of the Women's Liberation Movement can easily observe one of the effects of women's minority group thinking, which is to make them relatively unaware of their situation as a sex and gender-group. Awareness of 'sisterhood' is low and many women fail to see just how they are discriminated against as women.

Of course, the biological differences between the sexes may have some bearing on the parallel differences in personality types. The problem is one of proving any connection between biology and personality, and of giving a convincing explanation of the impact one has upon the other.

Some lines of enquiry have been started. Two researchers have found, for example, that newborn females are significantly higher than newborn males in basal skin conductance (that is, the degree to which their skin will conduct electricity). They are more sensitive to pain and show more immediate and marked responses to physical changes—the removal of a covering blanket, airjet stimulation of the abdomen —than do males. Does this tie in with their greater avoidance of physical aggression from childhood on? If so how? The assumption of course is that the further back one can go in demonstrating the existence of sex differences, the more likely they are to be innate. But is it possible that even these sex differences in the newborn could be some sort of early response to sex-differentiated culture? Though this suggestion may sound outrageous, further research on basal skin conductance among newborn children showed that second and later children have a significantly higher skin conductance than firstborn, independently of their sex. If the mechanism here is a physiological one, it is a very mysterious one indeed. As an alternative explanation, differences in parental handling of second and later babies compared to first are known to exist.

It is also possible to hark back to hormones as an explanatory factor. Although there is no sex difference in the newborn baby's secretion of hormones, the brain is probably one of the parts of the body which are differentiated by sex during the development of the foetus, under the control of the hormones (see Chapter 1). Harry Harlow, in his studies of animal behaviour, has demonstrated the sex differential in the aggressive play of young monkeys, and this has been associated to some extent with hormonal influences. He has described how male monkeys engage in more aggressive and threatening physical play than females, and more often take the initiative. In particular, the 'threat' response (stiffening of posture, baring the teeth etc) is much more common in males than females. (The human equivalent of the threat response is unprovoked aggression.) Male monkeys threaten both males and females, whereas females seldom threaten males and threaten other females only half as often as the males threaten the females. The particular value of the Harlows' experiments lies in the fact that these monkeys were reared by inanimate surrogate mothers who were not in a position to transmit culture to their infants. It is interesting that female monkeys reared in this fashion differed from females reared by monkey-mothers in their use of the threat response.

The latter are likely to present sexually (invite intercourse) when threatened by a male: the former threaten the male instead of presenting to him. With the large differences in size and strength between adult males and females this is a suicidal act, and it seems possible that monkey culture trains the female in the substitution of sexuality for aggression. The parallel in human culture is obvious.

(This example prompts the suggestion that the way in which learning can affect aggressive behaviour in animals has been neglected. One researcher has shown that aggressive behaviour in animals is significally dependent on how it is reinforced: mice and dogs can be trained to relative passivity by altering the type of reinforcement that aggressive behaviour is usually given.)

The general controversy about whether sex differences in personality and behaviour are innate or learned will probably rage fiercely for many years to come. As it is, it is obvious that culture plays an important part in the shaping of male and female personality, and nowhere is this more clearly demonstrated than in the cross-cultural evidence. On the other hand, it seems possible that biology may indicate the *direction* of the difference, although not its extent. Dr John Money, who has done important research on the social-sexual identity of people who are biologically intersexual (and who does not believe that we can equate biological maleness with aggressiveness or biological femaleness with passivity and dependence on the basis of the present evidence concerning either animals or humans) has this to say in general:

' The simple dichotomy of innate versus acquired is conceptually outdated in analysis of the developmental differentiation of femininity and masculinity, which is not to say that one should obliterate the distinction between genetics and environment. Rather, one needs the concept of a genetic norm of reaction that defines limits within which genetics may interact with envirnoment and, vice versa, of an environmental norm of reaction that defines limits within which environment may interact with genetics. **,**

3

Sex and intellect

It used to be a tradition among anti-feminists that the smaller size of the female brain was proof of woman's inferior intelligence. It is true that the average circumference of male heads exceeds that of female heads at all ages, but head circumference has no known intellectual correlates. Brain size does, however, bear a direct relationship to body size, and the female's brain is smaller than the male's because females are on average smaller than males. (Actually, ounce for ounce, the female has a slightly bigger brain than the male.)

If we want to investigate the relationship between intelligence and biological sex we must discard the idea of intelligence as a single quality, because existing tests of general intelligence have been standardised to minimise the known sex differences in composite abilities. Items which differentiate consistently between the sexes are never included. (This is the reverse procedure from the one used in the Masculinity-Femininity Test described in Chapter 2.) One significant fact which does emerge from tests of general intelligence is the tendency for girls to score higher in the early years (particularly before six) and boys higher later on (particularly after puberty). The results of tests administered over a period of time in late adolescence and adulthood to the same sample show a fairly consistent tendency for men to improve their scores relative to the women in the sample.

If we break intelligence down into components, sex differences emerge in the following abilities: verbal ability, number ability, spatial ability, creativity and analytic ability.

Verbal ability is a feminine speciality, particularly in the years before formal education begins. Girls speak sooner than boys, use longer sentences earlier and are generally more articulate. Girls learn to read sooner, and more boys than girls need remedial teaching in reading. Detailed studies of verbal ability show that the female advantage can be precisely located: in tests of verbal comprehension and verbal reasoning the sex differences are negligible, but in word fluency and language usage the girls are distinctly better. Thus the female superiority in verbal ability should properly be called linguistic, since it is in speech and communication that females excel.

The primary sex difference in vocabulary is ironed out by the age of five or six when boys catch up with girls, but the sex difference in reading skills remains until the age of ten. In tests of grammar, spelling and word fluency, boys never catch up with girls, who excel in these areas throughout the school years.

In number ability, there appear to be no sex differences in the early years. Gesell's observations tend to show a slight superiority among the girls; but later in school life boys do better than girls on tests of numerical/arithmetical reasoning, though on tests of computation the girls are better. After the age of eleven the male's ability to perform well on tasks of arithmetical reasoning becomes consistent and marked. Figure 6 shows the distribution of scores on an arithmetical reasoning test undertaken by eight and nine-year-olds. Other studies show less of a difference than this one—but the diagram serves as a good illustration of how, on any such distribution, the majority of individuals fall within the same range of scores, regardless of sex.

Sex differences in creativity differ according to how the term 'creative' is defined. On aesthetic appreciation in music and fine art, females excel: however, there is direct evidence that this is because of the different training males and females receive in artistic subjects. Another meaning of 'creativity' has been investigated by a test which asks children to think of ways in which toys could be improved. On the whole males appear as more inventive. Up to about seven, children of both sexes score better on toys appropriate to their own sex: after seven, boys are able to think of more ways of improving both masculine and feminine toys.

A more fundamental meaning of creativity involves the ability to 'break set' or restructure a problem in a new way—allowing the subject to show his or her

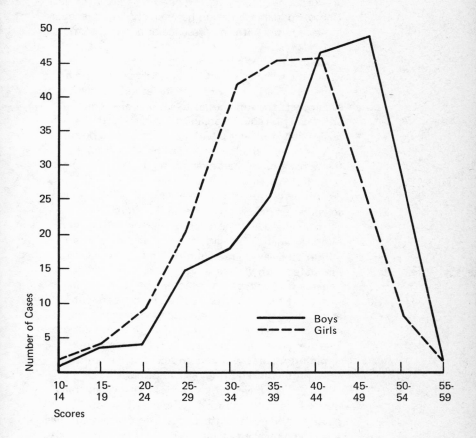

50 —
45 —
40 —
35 —
30 —
25 —
20 —
15 —
10 —
5 —

Number of Cases

10- 15- 20- 25- 30- 35- 40- 45- 50- 55-
14 19 24 29 34 39 44 49 54 59

Scores

——— Boys
– – – Girls

6   Distribution of scores by sex on a test of arithmetical reasoning. The mean score of the boys is 40.39 and that of the girls 35.81. It can be seen that nearly all individuals in both sex groups fall within the same range of scores.

originality. This is closely related to some component of analytic ability (and is also associated with arithmetical reasoning ability—hence perhaps the not unusual conjunction of mathematical and musical abilities in the same person.) In tests measuring this type of analytic ability, the ease with which a subject breaks set has been found to be associated with the kind of spatial orientation he or she has. In particular it is associated with the presence or absence of 'field dependence'.

An example of a field dependence test is one in which the subject is confronted with a chair and a room which are both tilted at angles independently of each other: the subject has to set one of them upright. This requires an ability to disregard misleading visual cues, and males tend to be better at this test than females, although the scores equalise if the females close their eyes. In general females show more field dependence than males.

This perceptual trait is a relatively stable one, and so is the sex difference correlated with it. It has been confirmed in Dutch, French, Italian and Hong Kong samples. There is also a tendency for differences within each sex on masculinity-femininity scales to be associated with variations in the extent of field dependence, so that, for example, more masculine men score high in the analytic field-independent approach, and the less masculine among them have a more characteristically female field-dependent score. The same relationship exists between masculinity-femininity scores within each sex, and the ability to solve problems requiring restructuring.

Other tests have found females to excel generally only where tasks call for the rapid perception of detail and frequent shifts of attention. These abilities tend to be relevant to tasks which are concerned with ways of grouping different objects or pictures. People who group on the basis of some selected elements the pictures have in common tend to be males, if the subjects are over the age of about seven. Males have also been shown to be less influenced by background stimuli (either irrelevant details in the pictures or outside distractions such as noises). Females are more aware of any stimuli, whether connected or unconnected with the task in hand.

Tests of analytic ability, therefore, show (1) that the spatial abilities and orientations of males and females tend to differ, and (2) that the ability of people to concentrate single-mindedly on a particular task tends to be differentiated by sex.

The differences in spatial orientation have been generally confirmed. For example, Erik Erikson has observed that boys and girls playing with toys differ in the use they make of space. Erikson confronted three hundred children aged ten to twelve with the task of 'constructing' a scene with toys on a table. He gave each one the same toys and tested him or her three times in the space of two years. He saw that the configurations boys and girls made with the toys differed: the girls' orientation emphasised what he named 'inner space' and that of the boys 'outer space'. To test whether the qualities he believed he detected had an objective existence that could be recognised by other observers, he asked other people to sort photographs of the toy scenes into male and female piles, using his criteria: the correlation between his own evaluation and those of the other observers was in fact statistically significant. The assessments also correlated with the actual sexes of the children who had done the tests.

Erikson defines the typical 'male' and 'female' configuration:

❛ ...the girls' scene is an *interior* scene, represented either as a configuration of furniture without any surrounding walls, or by a *simple enclosure* built with blocks. In the girls' scene, people and animals are mostly *within* such an interior or enclosure, and they are primarily people or animals in a *static* (sitting, standing) position. Girls' enclosures consist of *low walls,* i.e. only one block high, except for an occasional elaborate *doorway.* These interiors of houses with or without walls were, for the most part expressly peaceful...

Boys' scenes are either houses with *elaborate walls* or *facades with protrusions* such as cones or cylinders representing ornaments or cannons. There are *high towers;* and there are *exterior scenes.* In boys' constructions more people and animals are *outside* enclosures or buildings, and there are more *automotive objects* and *animals moving* along streets and intersections. There are elaborate automotive *accidents,* but also traffic channeled or arrested by the *policeman.* While high structures are prevalent, in the configurations of the boys, there is also much play with the danger of collapse or *downfall;* ruins were exclusively boys' constructions.

The male and female spaces, then, were dominated respectively by height and downfall and by strong motion and its channelisation or arrest; and by static interiors which were open or simply enclosed, and peaceful or intruded upon. **❯**

Not surprisingly, Erikson, as a psychoanalyst, considers that this different use of space by males and females is a reflection of their anatomy. In his view the inner space (womb) of girls and outer space (penis) of boys is a factor of irremediable importance to them, moulding their orientation to space outside their own bodies and creating a different awareness of space itself.

The sex difference in spatial orientation as described by Erikson seems to echo the difference in analytic ability found in tests of field dependence. In Erikson's play constructions, males were characterised by the use of height, downfall, strong movement and its channelisation and arrest; females by the enclosure of static interiors. In the 'chair and room' test, the female's relative inability to distinguish between the positions of the chair and the room shows a field-dependent approach that seems to have something in common with the girls' predilection for the static and the enclosed in the play-construction scenes. The male's sharper perception of the relationship between horizontal and vertical planes in the 'chair and room' test correspondingly suggests the exploratory use of space visible in Erikson's play scenes, so that both these experiments may demonstrate the same characteristic difference in spatial orientation between the sexes in our culture.

Measured IQ is one thing: demonstrated intellectual achievement is another. Throughout school life girls achieve better results than boys, and generally do better in examinations. If this intellectual achievement is compared with aptitudes for specific subjects, it is clear that girls do better even in subjects where boys tend to have the greater aptitude. This difference is usually attributed to the superior linguistic ability of girls (a factor which is related to memory).

Yet, despite the generally higher achievement of girls at school, there is a curious disparity between the achievement of individual girls and their measured IQ. (With boys, the disparity tends to be between achievements and aptitudes in specific subjects.) Many studies reveal a closer relationship between achievement and measured IQ for boys than for girls, and this disparity extends beyond school life: one follow-up study of gifted children revealed *no relationship* between the level of occupational achievement and measured IQ for girls, though there was a substantial correlation for boys. Another study of gifted children followed through to adulthood showed a close relationship between IQ and occupational level for the men but virtually no relationship for the women, although both had started in the same high IQ range as children. The occupations of the adult women were undistinguished. Two thirds of those with IQ's of 170 or above were housewives or office workers. At adolescent and adult levels the women in this sample were also subject to a greater drop in IQ than were the men. Girls thus seem particularly prone to 'under-achievement' in relation to their measured IQ.

Since there are these disparities between intellectual achievement on the one hand and specific aptitudes and measured intelligence on the other,

85

what does this suggest? The former finding indicates that the linguistic-verbal component in intellectual achievement is considerable (and favours girls); whereas the latter indicates that external factors influence the conversion of measured intelligence into intellectual achievement (which favours boys).

Female under-achievement usually begins around puberty, while the (less frequent) male under-achievement characteristically begins earlier. The decline in girls' achievement takes place at a time when the hormonal differentiation between the sexes is accelerated, but this is also the time when each sex is being initiated into important aspects of its adult role. In the male role, achievement is stressed: in the female role, conformity. The result of this is a double bind for the girls: they may be both intellectually able and eager to do well academically (and they are still pressed to do well by the school) but they are keenly aware of the fact that the adult female role embraces lower academic ability and achievement than the male. This, together with the boys' overt behaviour towards them, leads them to fear that if they continue to 'achieve' they will do so at the price of losing their femininity—their popularity with boys.

This double bind hypothesis is not just specula-tion: it is confirmed by empirical studies. For example, Joyce Joseph's account of the attitudes to work and marriage of six hundred adolescent girls shows how these girls have acquired traditional female expectations about their future roles. In the age range fourteen to seventeen, the vast majority have no ambition or expected achievement other than marriage and homemaking. They certainly do not expect to found a 'career' on their school achieve-ments, as the boys do. The question 'What will be your job?' (which was slanted towards paid employ-ment) get the answer 'marriage' from 48% of the sample. In essays written on the topic of their future lives, 90% talked about marriage, while 53% mentioned paid work (to be distinguished from 'achievement') as something that would incur their husbands' wrath ('My husband insisted I gave up

A married woman works on the interior design of a freighter in East Germany.
(Fotolink)

work') or as a way of saving money to buy a house, rarely as a satisfying means of personal fulfilment.

Another relevant investigation was made (by Aileen Schoeppe) into sex differences in the socialisation of adolescents. It distinguished five 'developmental tasks' facing adolescents: (1) learning an adult sex role (2) achieving independence from parents (3) developing conscience and moral values (4) getting along with age mates and (5) developing intellectual skills. All five of these distinguished between males and females, revealing the much more crucial role of autonomy and self-directiveness to the male, while the girl is under pressure to develop the less exciting quality of conformity. In this investigation boys who accepted their sex role overtly seemed to accept it covertly also, while girls did not—suggesting some (successfully repressed) antagonism on their part to the culturally approved female role.

Conformity and domesticity, either real or anticipated, would appear to militate against the values of academic achievement for the female. Females themselves may be very aware of this conflict. One American study reported that over half a sample of 163 American college women pretended to be intellectually inferior to their boy friends, 14% very often and 43% sometimes. An earlier study conducted elsewhere in the United States came up with comparable figures, suggesting that the habit is widespread. As the author of this study suggests, the double bind which leads to female under-achievement is a result of the conflict of two disparate roles. On the one hand, the role demanding academic achievement for women partly obliterates the differentiation by sex: on the other, the felt need to be popular with males is a facet of a strictly feminine role, which involves dependence rather than independence. (Boys who are popular with peers tend to be independent while popular girls are dependent.) As a result of conforming to this latter role, females of any age beyond puberty find it difficult to escape from traditional notions of female inferiority.

Ideas of feminine inferiority in intellectual

achievement, therefore, still hold sway, but they cannot entirely explain the gap between male and female performance. Other findings link the female's academic performance with qualities of feminine personality, and what is significant is that these qualities correlate with intellectual achievement (and failure to achieve) in both sexes.

Let us take two examples of the connection between intellectual performance and feminine personality.

First, females seem to be relatively unable to evaluate their own abilities realistically. In a test in which children are asked how well they expect to do on a new task, boys believe that it is their own abilities that will bring them success, and a boy's estimate of his chances tends to be in proportion to his measured IQ. The same is not true of girls, who tend to believe that their achievement is more a matter of chance.

Secondly, females appear to be more afraid of failure than males and more disorganised by it. Boys rise to an intellectual challenge, girls retreat from it. A study of children aged three to nine found that when they could choose whether to return to tasks they had previously failed at or to tasks on which they had already succeeded, girls more often chose the latter and boys the former. This reaction persists as a ritualised response in later years, so that a group of university women were found to be less able to perform a difficult task if they were told they were doing badly on it.

The inability to judge one's performance realistically, and the disruptive fear of failure, are qualities which lead to lowered achievement. They are also qualities more often found in females than males in our culture, but males who do suffer from them are subject to impaired achievement in exactly the same way. If we look further into the origins of achievement, we find that both high intellectual achievement itself and also a close correlation between achievement and measured IQ are, *in males and females alike,* associated with (1) *a general lack of dependency,* and (2) *a childhood identification with the father.* This interesting pair of findings is of course of great significance in the debate about the origin of sex differences in intellectual functioning. It suggests that these differences are very closely associated with sex differences in personality, and if these in turn are not determined by primarily biological factors—which seems doubtful in view of the evidence discussed in Chapter 2—then sex differences in intelligence are not likely to be determined by them either.

In 1943 David Levy showed how the male children of over-protective, dependency-encouraging mothers resembled females in school achievement and intellectual ability. These boys were better in vocabulary and reading ability than 'normal' boys and inferior in arithmetical and scientific ability and achievement. Levy suggested that this lessening of intellectual masculinity was due to close association with the mother. Since then, the hypothesis that the verbal superiority of girls (and over-protected males) is due to intimacy with the mother has not been supported by the little evidence we have (though it has not been disproved either). However, the relationship Levy observed between dependence on the mother and relative lack of analytic ability has now been confirmed. In this area, which most consistently differentiated between the sexes, Witkin and his associates (who have been responsible for much of the research into it) have shown that field dependence and inability to break set are correlated with dependency in interpersonal relations, suggesti-bility, conformity and lack of self-reliance in both males and females. The finding that more females than males are field-dependent and under-achieve in relation to their measured IQ does not therefore suggest a relationship between intelligence and biological factors. It suggests, instead, a relationship between personality and maleness or femaleness; but unless it can be shown that this relationship is biologically determined in some way, it cannot be used to show that sex differences in intellectual achievement and spatial orientation are independent of culture and learning.

Can we connect the qualities of personality associated with under-achievement and field dependence in both sexes with particular features of maternal behaviour that inhibit independence in male and female children?

The behaviour of mothers towards girls engaged in problem solving has been watched. It seem that the mothers of those who are good at spatial tasks leave their children alone to solve problems by themselves: mothers of girls who are poor at spatial tasks are intrusive: they offer suggestions, praise the child for performing well and criticise her for performing poorly. (The latter group of girls, incidentally, also tend to be more highly verbal.) While the mother's behaviour may be a response to the child's own difficulties, her expectations may also affect the child's potential by transmitting a fear of failure and lack of self-confidence. Mothers may respond in this way to female children because they identify with them more closely than with males, and perhaps project onto them their own fear of failure and lack of confidence; if they do, these features of female behaviour are likely to be perpetuated over generations. Other research has shown how the crucial factor generating independence in girls—and thus intellectual achievement—is 'freedom to wander and explore', an absence of maternal restrictiveness.

In fact the correlation between independence and analytic ability is often *higher* for males than females. For example, a study of personality factors associated with progressive increases in IQ found that independence was a factor for both sexes, but that the relationship was stronger for boys. It may well be, therefore, that the more independent upbringing that boys tend to receive is one reason for the male's superiority in analytic reasoning.

The other quality of personality which has emerged as critical in the study of intellectual functioning is really a complex of qualities deriving from the kind of identification a child builds up with his or her parents. In both boys and girls, identification with the father is a correlate of high intellectual achievement.

Most tests of masculinity-femininity, such as the one devised by Terman and Miles, show that brighter males score higher on femininity and lower on masculinity than their less intelligent peers. Brighter females score higher on masculinity, but on the other hand they also score higher on femininity. Here masculinity seem to be equated with 'dominance' and 'motivation to achieve': 'femininity' with relatively 'adult' behaviour (the opposite of childishness). This type of male 'femininity' and female 'masculinity' does not refer to the sexuality of individuals, but to the extent to which they share the interests and activities of the other sex. Using this definition of cross-sex identification, a reseacher studying sex differences in analytic ability found that males who scored high on an embedded figures test (that is, one in which the subject has to find a particular simple figure within a larger complex one) had identified with their mothers rather than their fathers. Females with high analytic ability had identified with their fathers. An earlier study of the autobiographies of female mathematicians showed the same attachment to the interests and activities of their fathers. Studies of children relating general measures of IQ to interest in the activities of the opposite sex have found that bright girls are more likely to enjoy boys' games than girls'.

A fascinating explanation of the importance of sex role identification in the development of analytic ability has been given by David Lynn.

Lynn takes it as axiomatic that the development of masculinity and femininity in children is achieved by the process of identification—that is, by internalising the masculine or feminine role of the relevant parent. He says that the female's identification with her mother is equivalent, in terms of learning, to a 'lesson', while that of the male with his father is a 'problem'. The two are different because the environment in which children are brought up is sexually asymetrical: both sexes are reared by the mother, while the father is absent at work for much of the time. The little boy thus has to 'break set'—to discard his dependence on females (mother, nursery teacher) and identify with the relatively 'external' masculinity which his work-absent father represents. Lynn explains:

❝ The little girl acquires a learning method which primarily involves: (a) a personal relationship and (b) imitation rather than restructuring the field and abstracting principles. On the other hand the little boy acquires a different learning method which primarily involves (a) defining the goal (b) restructuring the field; and (c) abstracting principles. ❞

So the male acquires his analytic ability the hard way: in taking up his masculine role he has, as a first step, to make use of a problem-solving, field-restructuring principle.

Lynn's hypothesis has some evidence to support it, for instance Levy's finding that overprotected male children who had not identified with their fathers in the normal way resembled females in their intellectual orientation. Lynn does not suggest that girls, too, may develop their problem-solving abilities through identification with their fathers—indeed, he uses his idea to explain sex differences in intellectual ability. But perhaps the cross-sex identification of intellectually achieving females carries the same implication? Females who identify with the interests and activities of males may have restructured the field in the same way, though not with entirely the same consequences. In getting beyond the relationship with the mother and cultivating in themselves aspects of the father's role, both sexes are making themselves independent of their immediate perceptual field. This is confirmed by an analysis of the sex differences in problem solving. The sex differences are only significant when the task involves the overcoming of a context—that is, breaking set.

93   This fits with the evidence which shows that the most impressive sex difference in intellectual achievement emerge at stages where the pressure on girls to conform to the feminine role is greatest. Girls aged five to ten are less 'feminine' in their interests and in the activities they prefer than they come to be in later years: they differentiate less than boys do between masculine and feminine activities. However as puberty approaches and is passed, the following things happen: (1) there is a considerable pressure (from parents, teachers, peers and boys) to act 'feminine' (2) achievement goes down (3) the correlation between achievement and IQ goes down too. In other words, as identification with females and 'femininity' increases, girls become more feminine in their intellectual orientation. Witkin and his colleagues comment, in their review of sex differences, that their finding of greater field dependence in the female cannot be demonstrated at ages younger than eight. There is some evidence that there are no significant sex differences in this younger age group, as there are also none in the very old. The period of greatest field dependence in females is young adulthood, when the differentiation of roles between the sexes is at its height.

These explanations of intellectual differences between the sexes concentrate on the effect of upbringing. There are also some explanations based on biological factors which carry some weight.

The general time-tables of development of boys and girls differ, so that one would expect the development of intelligence and achievement to show a different pattern in each sex. Each advance in childhood has to wait until the relevant physical structures are complete—a three-year-old cannot fold paper diagonally, but a four-year-old can. In general, sex differences in the development of intelligence during childhood keep in step with physiological development. Thus girls talk earlier because the brain structures necessary to speech tend to mature earlier in girls. But physiology does not explain either the differences in spatial ability, which are the most enduring sex differences in intelligence, or the fluctuating correlations between measured IQ and intellectual achievement, for which we clearly need a different kind of explanation.

One theory, so far unvalidated, suggests that the intellectual performance of girls is more closely controlled by genetics than is that of boys, which is more vulnerable to the impact of environment. Resemblances in IQ between parents and children set in earlier in girls than boys (boys catch up by the age of six) and early maternal behaviour seems to have a more lasting influence on the IQ scores of boys than of girls. Bayley and Schaeffer, whose theory this is, have shown by a reanalysis of data on adopted children, that the correlation of adopted children's IQs with those of their natural parents is significant for girls but not for boys.

Dr John Money, in his invaluable work on intersexuality in America, claims to have discovered a component of intelligence that is under specific genetic control. Like colour blindness, a disability he calls 'space-form blindness' appears to be linked to genes located on the X chromosome. It affects people who have one of the two sex chromosomes missing (they have the designation XO) and among such people Money has found a strong tendency for non-verbal intelligence to be much lower than verbal intelligence (overall intelligence is about normal). Both verbal IQ and verbal comprehension are high, but on performance IQ, freedom from distractibility, and perceptual organisation, the scores are low. These patients are relatively inept mechanically and unable to handle problems that involve finding logical relationships between spaces and shapes.

This particular relationship between a deficient chromosome constitution, and an intellectual disability is a special case. What do we conclude from it? Presumably, the correlation of these IQ patterns with the absence of one sex chromosome could be held to show that the intellect is to some extent genetically controlled by the sex chromosomes. On this theory, it was the absence of male hormone production in the critical period before birth that caused the central nervous system to develop according to the female pattern in these patients. (The fact that some of them had a predisposition towards biological maleness in one test—the chromatin test—is held to have been outweighed by the absence of the male Y chromosome.)

The speculation then follows that the chromosomes, through the mechanism of the hormones, produce sex-differences in cognition. However, against this one must add that the evidence on the sex differentiation of the central nervous system is not yet conclusive, and there is also the fact that all these chromosome-deficient individuals were reared as normal females (since their genitals had the normal female appearance). Thus they were subject to all the usual sex-typed expectations and pressures, and their pronounced female spatial-orientation patterns could have been moulded by culture and upbringing as much as those of any normal female are.

In general, the genetic mechanism for producing sex differences in intelligence, if there is such a mechanism, is unknown, although it is recognised that all children's intelligence is to some degree genetically inherited from their parents. This can be seen from studies of identical twins reared separately and together (though these studies show that environmental conditions also have a significant impact—a finding which is complementary rather than contradictory). One component of general intelligence—mechanical ability—which is closely related to spatial orientation and which is one of the intellectual traits observed to be lacking in XO chromosome individuals, seems to be genetically determined to some extent. Identical twins resemble each other much more closely in respect of this trait than fraternal twins, even when the members of each pair of twins are reared in the same home conditions.

But most theories which argue from observed differences in ability to the existence of innate differences under genetic control lack supporting evidence and are purely speculative, whether the differences they aim to account for are between individuals or between sexes. Such theories confuse specific findings and hypothetical explanations. They also frequently omit a description of the exact mechanism which is supposed to operate in producing the differences in question.

Erikson's account of the sex differences in children's play construction is a case in point; although he does not actually say that the differences are innate, the intimate association between them and body ground-plan means that he is giving a general biological explanation. The words he underlines in the description of the girls' constructions refer to the female's relegation to interior, domestic, sedentary occupations in our society. In the boys' constructions, the underlined words refer to activity, aggression, self-projection, exteriority and male pursuits. When faced with this result, the question he asks is 'Does the anatomy of male and female suggest a difference along these lines?' The question he fails to ask is 'How do boys and girls translate this anatomical difference into such detailed and specific differences of activity and interest?' An even more pertinent question is 'Why do these differences so exactly parallel the roles society defines for male and female?' The children in Erikson's sample had had ample time to observe these differences between male and female roles, and ample time to incorporate them into their own play. Aged between ten and twelve, they were far too old to be used for studying the possibility of innate sex differences.

The kind of interpretation Erikson offers has been very influential. Witkin and his associates, who have been responsible for most of the work on sex differences in spatial perception, considered it in 1954; but in 1962 they came down in favour of 'social pressures', emphasising the often neglected fact that most differences between the sexes, although statistically significant, are not as great as the individual differences within each sex. So the differences in perception between males and females are small compared to the differences found between one woman and another, and one man and another.

Obviously what we need is an investigation into th patterns of intelligence prevailing in other cultures, together with an analysis of the intellectual aptitudes of each sex, where these exist. We also need a study of the relationship between intelligence and personality in other societies, since this relationship has been one of the most interesting things to emerge from research in our own society.

An intelligent guess might be that such an investigation would not demonstrate the presence of universal sex differences in intelligence. We may also guess that this negative conclusion would be due as much to the variation in masculine and feminine patterns of personality between different cultures as it would be to the tremendous variation in individual endowment among human beings generally.

4
Sexuality

As a leading anthropologist once observed, 'sex' is not a particularly useful word in the analysis of cultures. To survive, a culture must reproduce, and copulation is the only way. But what is defined as 'sexual' in content or implication varies infinitely from one culture to another or within the same culture in different historical periods.

In Victorian times for instance, a large group of Western females were denied their sexuality altogether, but the twentieth century has seen the emergence (or re-emergence, after the inhibitions of the eighteenth and nineteenth centuries) of the female's right to sexuality, which has come to be defined at least partly in terms of her own sexual needs. The Victorian lady was not supposed to have sexual desires—hence her paradoxical use as a sexual object for the man's satisfaction. Her twentieth-century counterpart, however, has considerable auras of sexuality, extending beyond the bedroom into an entire world of commercially-oriented sex and erotic meaning.

These terms 'sex' and 'sexual' are subject to constant confusion. The dictionary gives, under 'sexual', 'Of, pertaining to, or based on, sex or the sexes, or on the distinction of sexes; pertaining to generation or copulation'. Perhaps it is not surprising that the confusion exists: 'sex' (biological maleness or femaleness) and 'sexuality' (behaviour related to copulation) are very closely connected. Behaviour is 'sexual' if it refers to the kind of relationship between male and female in which copulation is, or could be, or is imagined to be, a factor. 'Sexuality' describes the whole area of personality related to sexual behaviour.

Both male and female must have some propensity for sexual behaviour if copulation is to occur, but this propensity is usually held to be different in male and female. Along with the male's greater aggression in other fields, goes his aggression in the sphere of sexuality: males initiate sexual contact, and take the symbolically, if not actually, aggressive step of vaginal penetration—a feat which is possible even with a frigid mate. They assume the dominant position in intercourse. Males ask females to go to bed with them, or marry them, or both: not vice versa.

The female's sexuality is supposed to lie in her receptiveness and this is not just a matter of her open vagina: it extends to the whole structure of feminine personality as dependent, passive, unaggressive and submissive. Female sexuality has been held to involve long arousal and slow satisfaction, inferior sex drive, susceptibility to field dependence (a crying child distracts the attention) and romantic idealism rather than lustful reality. Women are psychologically, no less than anatomically, incapable of rape.

That these stereotypes persist can be seen from any woman's magazine and almost any fiction dealing with sexual relationships. Many men and women conform to them in reality, as can be seen from the kind of psychological problems each sex has over its sexuality. (The incompetence of some women in taking contraceptive precautions often comes from the fact that they do not want, or are not able, to direct the course of their own sexuality: they feel that to admit they are planning—even perhaps, that they desire—to make love is immoral; and immoral can still mean 'unladylike' or 'unfeminine' despite the decease of the Victorian era.)

What do we know about the sex drive in men and women, about the physiological processes involved in copulation and orgasm? Are we able to say that in these things men and women are biologically different?

Since 1954, William Masters and Virginia Johnson have been studying the sexual response of the human male and female, from a scientific point of view. After studying the sexual response of 382 women aged from eighteen to seventy-eight and 312 men aged from twenty-one to eighty-nine, they wrote an account of the differences and similarities in the male and female response to sexual tension. In this account, they described four phases that are discernible in the sexual responses of both male and female: the excitement phase, the plateau phase, the

EXCITEMENT PHASE

nipple erection (30%)

nipple erection
sex-tension flush (25%)

PLATEAU PHASE

sex-tension flush (25%)
carpopedal spasm
generalised skeletal muscle tension
hyperventilation
tachycardia (100 to 160/min)

sex-tension flush (75%)
carpopedal spasm
generalised skeletal muscle tension
hyperventilation
tachycardia (100 to 160/min)

ORGASMIC PHASE

specific skeletal muscle contractions
hyperventilation
tachycardia (100 to 180/min)

specific skeletal muscle contractions
hyperventilation
tachycardia (110 to 180/min)

RESOLUTION PHASE

sweating reaction (30 to 40%)
hyperventilation
tachycardia (150 to 180/min)

sweating reaction (30 to 40%)
hyperventilation
tachycardia (150 to 180/min)

TABLE 7 General body reactions in sexual response. Male responses are shown in the left-hand column, female on the right. (Carpopedal spasm = involuntary contraction of muscles in the wrist and foot; hyperventilation = rapid breathing causing an excess of carbon dioxide in the blood; tachycardia = fast heart rate.)

orgasmic phase and the resolution phase.

In the first phase, excitement may develop in male or female in response to any kind of sexual stimulation, psychical or physical. Sexual stimulation produces erection in the males, taking from three to eight seconds, and vaginal lubrication in the female, which becomes well-established in between five and fifteen seconds. These are the first responses, and if the excitement phase is prolonged, both may disappear.

In the second, plateau phase, the degree of sexual tension becomes intense in both sexes. There is both superficial and deep vasocongestion (filling of the blood vessels) in the pelvic organs and throughout the entire body. The ability to respond to minor non-sexual stimuli may be lost. If effective stimulation is discontinued at this point, a long and frustrating resolution phase without orgasm is likely in both male and female.

In the orgasmic phase, orgasm proceeds with between eight and ten contractions of the relevant organs in both male and female, though the female's continue for longer. About 50% of females are capable of having a further orgasm immediately, while this is true of only a very few males.

In the resolution phase, following orgasm, the physiological signs of sex-tension dissipate either slowly if excitement in the first phase built up slowly, or rapidly if the ascent to orgasm was a short-lived experience. There is no relation in either sex between the type of stimulation and the intensity or duration of response. The physiological reactions are the same for intercourse, masturbation or fantasy. The similarities in the general body reactions of male and female during sexual response are shown in Table 7.

Kinsey, in his 'Sexual Behaviour in the Human Female' made a similar comparison between male and female cycles of sexual response. In particular, he observed that the anatomical differences between the sexes were not of much relevance here, since the clitoris is equipped with a system of sensory nerves as numerous and as extensive as those of the penis, if not more so. Kinsey said:

❛ The labia minora and the vestibule of the vagina provide more extensive sensitive areas in the female than are to be found in any homologous structure of the male. Any advantage which the larger size of the male phallus may provide is equalled or surpassed by the greater extension of the tactilely sensitive areas in the female genitalia. ❜

In considering the physiology of sexual response, he observed that there were no discernible differences, that females seem to be able to reach orgasm as quickly as males, and that 'The usual statement that the female is slower in her capacity to reach orgasm is unsubstantiated by any data which we have been able to secure'.

He concluded: 'In spite of the widespread and oft repeated emphasis on the supposed differences between female and male sexuality, we fail to find any anatomical or physiologic basis for such differences.'

It was also Kinsey who observed that during masturbation a woman takes the same length of time to reach an orgasm as a man does—between two and four minutes. This stands in strange contradiction to the wealth of evidence we have that many women are unable to reach orgasm in intercourse, and suggests (as do the Masters and Johnson data) a physiological identity of sexual reaction in male and female which is somehow lost or distorted by conditioning.

To Kinsey we are indebted for the basic research which enables us to relate the apparent differences in the ability of the two sexes to reach orgasm to their very different patterns of experience.

Males reach their peak of sexual activity (as measured by the frequency of orgasm in coitus, masturbation and petting) three of four years after the beginning of puberty. The highest point of female sexual activity is reached much later, around thirty. Sexual activity in women tends to vary with their marital status. Masturbation increases with marriage,

103

with the rising age of the husband, and particularly with divorce or widowhood. In Kinsey's sample 28% of fifteen-year-old girls, 40% of those aged up to twenty, and 62% of those aged up to forty had masturbated. Between twenty and fifty the frequency of masturbation stabilises for women with relatively little variation. The much higher frequency of masturbation for men, which is not related to marital status, declines after the age of eighteen or twenty.

These differences in sexual experience are associated with, and help to explain, differences in ability to reach orgasm. The ability to respond sexually is at least partly a function of experience for both sexes, and as women begin all forms of sexual activity later than men—masturbation, petting with or without orgasm, and intercourse—they are slower to reach a 'masculine' level of sexual response. If the figures are adjusted to take account of the difference in experience of the two groups, their responses to sexual stimulation are very alike.

It is clear from these figures that women take longer than men to discover their sexual-genital excitability and they seem to need the aid of a male partner to do so. Does the more prolonged development of female genital sexuality occur because of the female's relative paucity of experience? Or is the paucity of experience a reflection of the slower and different maturation of the female's potential for being sexually aroused?

In 'The Sexual Behaviour of Young People' Michael Schofield relates the amount of sexual experience boys and girls have had, and the age at which they began, to their family situation. He finds that in general girls are more closely controlled by the family, and allowed far fewer opportunities to get sexual experience than boys. Mostly the girls are more emotionally bound up with their families than the boys: they set a higher value on loyalty to the family and on conforming to parental norms of behaviour.

A comparison of the sexually experienced girl with the sexually experienced boy shows that

experience	male	female
no experience	69	37
petting	82	53
petting with orgasm	78	74

(male = male students, no 931
female = female students, no 337)

TABLE 8 This table shows the percentage of people with different degrees of sexual experience who wished to have coitus. (None of them had actually experienced it.)

❝ ...experienced girls have gone much farther than boys in rejecting family influences. Relations with both parents were often strained, and they were less likely to receive advice on sexual matters from their parents, and when they did get this advice, they were more likely to reject it.

In matters of parental discipline the experienced girls were like the experienced boys. These girls did not tell their parents where they were going, did not have to be in at a definite time; spent more time outside the home...Like the boys, their home situation provided them with more opportunities and facilities for sexual activities. **❞**

In other words, the home situation of the average girl is a much more restricting influence on the development of sexual behaviour than that of the average boy. To approach the level of sexual experience boys reach, a girl has positively to reject the influence of home and family.

So it is not surprising to find that most female deviance in adolescence consists of sexual offences (which is not true of boys). Somewhere between two thirds and three quarters of all female acts of delinquency are sexual. Also, while most of the sex offences committed by adolescent males involve sexual deviations, female offences are promiscuous but otherwise normal (that is, they are concerned with heterosexual intercourse).

This lead to various conclusions. (1) Parents' expectations of appropriate behaviour in the adolescent girl exclude overt sexual activity, whereas for the boy they permit it. (2) Parental controls (and social controls in general) retard the onset of sexual experience in most adolescent girls. (3) Where they do not, overt sexual activity is likely to be allied with delinquency (or defined as delinquency) because of the equation between femininity and the absence of overt sexual behaviour for the adolescent female. A rebellious girl may show her defiance by acts of overt sexuality; alternatively, active sexuality may be construed as deviation. In any case, both delinquency in general and sexual delinquency in particular are likely to be correlated with the girl's rejection of home and family. And this rejection is itself less likely in girls than in boys.

These findings clearly help to provide a cultural explanation of the apparent differences in male and female sexuality. What weight should we give to the opposing theory, held by many people, that, for biological reasons, sexuality arises spontaneously in the male but not in the female?

Puberty for the male is an overtly sexual event. Right from the beginning, his sexuality is localised in the genitals by the start of seminal emissions. Female puberty, on the other hand, is marked by the onset of menstruation, which has a reproductive rather than sexual significance, and brings with it associations of pain and probably fear. Within Western culture, sexuality may well be latent in the female, while manifest in the male. If so, this may be because females resist the open acknowledgement of their sexuality, and some backing for this belief comes from those cases in which females with glandular disturbances have clitoral erections when they are sexually aroused. When they are relieved of this by surgery, they claim pleasure at being able to feel like 'normal' women: clearly they have learnt to associate spontaneous sexuality with the aggressive masculine role.

But in other societies this difference between male and female sexuality is reduced to a mere linguistic quibble. The theory that male sexuality arises spontaneously and is specifically genital while the female's is not, is simply not borne out by the behaviour of males and females in other cultures—for instance by the Brazilian tribe studied by Jules Henry (see Chapter 2) or the Trobriand islanders studied by Malinowski (see below). The differences in the emotional meaning of puberty to male and female in our cultures, are not necessarily universal either, any more than are the social differences influencing the ways in which they gain their sexual experience.

Although there is a distinct difference between males and females in the physiological events and timing of puberty, these differences may be either accentuated or minimised by culture. As Michael Schofield shows, the onset of puberty in our culture not only produces a whole set of social responses from family and friends which differ between the sexes: it also arouses different expectations in the girls and boys themselves. For the girl, puberty is a time of danger from which she only emerges by tying herself to a single man in marriage (or at least in a relationship that will lead to marriage). For the male, on the other hand, it is a time of adventure, when the apron strings which tie him to the home are released as he sets out to prove his manhood. While pubescent male and pubescent female alike may feel the stirrings of a specifically sexual-genital excitement, and the consequent urge for its release, the female's thoughts are directed into anticipating the less dangerous occupations of wife, mother and housewife. Her dreams of two children, her own house and all the trappings of domesticity thus represent a 'displacement activity' whose function is the inhibition of the sexual urge. There is no equivalent inhibition acting on the male.

Because puberty is a bridge between childhood and adulthood, and because the adult roles of the sexes are significantly differentiated in our society both inside and outside the home, the climate in which male and female pass through puberty tends to stress rather than ignore sex differences in the physiological process itself. An additional factor is perhaps our cultural emphasis on the importance of sexuality. The Arapesh, who as a culture devalue sexuality and develop tenderness and parental responsibility in both males and females, do not treat the adolescent girl as in need of protection from the male's exploitation of her as a sexual object. Menstruation is therefore not the signal of danger it is in our society. Arapesh males simply do not regard females as vessels for their own sexual satisfaction, but as individuals whose desirability as spouses is related to the culture's primary work of child-rearing. The sexual feeling that exists between spouses is not fundamentally different from the other feelings or affections that tie siblings, or parents and children, together—it is just a more complete expression of it. In this context, adolescence is not a period of fervent mating choice either: by the age of nine or ten girls are already betrothed, and the adolescent male's task is to prepare his own betrothed for the responsibilities of parenthood which they will both share. The Arapesh have no fear that adolescents left to themselves will copulate, nor do the adolescents themselves expect that they will. Margaret Mead (in 'Sex and Temperament') explains:

‘ ...the Arapesh further contravene our traditional idea of men as spontaneously sexual creatures, and women as innocent of desire, until wakened, by denying spontaneous sexuality to both sexes and expecting the exceptions, when they do occur, to occur in women. Both men and women are conceived as merely capable of response to a situation that their society has already defined for them as sexual...with their definition of sex as response to an external stimulus rather than as spontaneous desire, both men and women are regarded as helpless in the face of seduction...Parents warn their sons even more than they warn their daughters against permitting themselves to get into situations in which someone can make love to them. ’

Puberty for the Arapesh is therefore hardly a physiological situation at all, although it remains a sign of maturation and of readiness for the adult role.

Anthropology shows that the whole area of human sexuality is subject to tremendous cultural variation. The following are among the many features of human sexual behaviour which vary: sexual play between children (which may be specifically genital and widely permitted throughout childhood, as among the Trobrianders, or heavily discouraged and repressed, in middle childhood especially, as in our own society); intercourse between immature adults (which may be a common occurrence unrelated to marriage and procreation, as in Samoa, or discouraged, as again in Western culture); the importance of sexual activity itself (which may be defined as the appropriate preoccupation for an entire society to the exclusion of other interests, as among the Truk, or may take a very secondary place indeed as among the Arapesh); the extent to which sexual desire is dangerous and needs curbing, as among the Manus, or is weak and uncertain and likely to fail altogether, as in Bali.

The idea that the female's sexuality is qualitatively different from the male's, and in particular that it is slow to mature and in need of intensive stimulation, is not universal in all cultures. In the Southwest Pacific society described by William Davenport (see Chapter 2) sexual intercourse is assumed to be highly pleasurable (and deprivation harmful) for both sexes. During the early years of marriage men and women are reported to have intercourse twice a day, with both reaching orgasm simultaneously. Intercourse is defined as a prolonged period of foreplay, during which there is a mutual genital stimulation by both partners, and a short period of copulation lasting fifteen to thirty seconds. It is firmly believed that, once stimulated during foreplay, neither male nor female can fail to reach orgasm, and women unable to reach orgasm are unheard of. Either husband or wife can break up the marriage if sexual intercourse is infrequent (that is, about every ten days).

In this society children beyond the age of three or four are discouraged from genital play, and all sex play between children is frowned upon: there is a latency period from about five or six until puberty when sexual behaviour is not in evidence. Beyond puberty and before marriage both males and females are urged to masturbate to orgasm in order to relieve sexual tension, which is assumed to be as great in females as in males.

Malinowski reported a similar convergence of male and female sexual behaviour among the Trobriand Islanders. Like many other people, the Trobrianders appear to do without latency—there is no period of childhood during which sexual interests and activities are absent. Small children play sexual games together; genital manipulation and oral genital stimulation are frequent. By the age of four or five children are mimicking intercourse, and girls of six to eight have intercourse with penetration. (This experience is delayed for boys, presumably until they are able to achieve full intercourse at the age of ten or twelve.) These sexual activities continue unabated throughout childhood, but at adolescence become more serious—the subject of great endeavour and absorbing preoccupation.

Trobriander folklore contains an account of ritual rape by women of men which the natives informed Malinowski was a regular occurrence. Since he was unable to observe it, he disbelieved them, but nevertheless acknowledged Trobriander women to be much more assertive and vigorous and stronger in their sexual drive than women of his own culture. The conventional invitation of female to male is erotic scratching, which draws blood. Malinowski wrote: 'On the whole, I think that in the rough usage of passion the woman is the more active. I have seen far larger scratches and marks on men than on women; and only women may actually lacerate their lovers.'

Amongst the Trobrianders, as also among the Lesu, Kurtatchi, Lepcha, Kwoma and Mataco, women frequently take the initiative in sexual relationships. Indeed, in the last two societies, sexual initiatives are taken by the female exclusively.

The positions used in intercourse by the Trobrianders omit the usual dorsal-ventral (man on top of woman) position used by Europeans—which they dislike because the women is hampered by the weight of the man and cannot be sufficiently active. The expression for orgasm means 'the seminal fluid discharge' and is used of both sexes, referring also to the nocturnal emission of seminal and glandular secretions in male and female. Masturbation is looked on by the Trobrianders as the practice of an idiot, one who is unable to indulge in heterosexual intercourse. It is unworthy of both men and women, whose proper sexuality is bound up with their mutual relationship. Malinowski, in comparing the sexuality of the Trobrianders with that of his own culture, concluded that there were qualitative differences between them. He said that the Trobriander threshhold of arousal was much higher than ours, and that sexual excitement was only produced in them by the direct stimulation of the sexual organs. Orgasm in both sexes needed more bodily contact, erotic preliminaries and direct stimulation—a characteristic which is usually considered to be specifically female in our culture.

The differences between the threshholds of arousal of men and women have been related to sexual differences in general in our society. The male is usually reported to be more often and more easily aroused—by visual stimuli or even by his own anticipation—than the female. The stimuli which arouse males and females will also, of course, normally be different, as will the type of erotic imagery accompanying it. Are there biological reasons for these differences?

Medical evidence suggests that the sex hormones may play a part in determining the threshhold and frequency of arousal. Children who undergo precocious puberty (because of a hormonal defect) sometimes have more frequent erotic dreams and daydreams, especially boys. Men who usually produce too little of the male hormones often become more sexually active with the administration of androgen, while women on androgen therapy also say that they feel increased sexual desire. Females masculinised before birth by an excess of male hormones, but reared as girls, are reported to exhibit an eroticism which is more characteristically male than female. Visual stimuli produce genital arousal in them, together with clitoral erection and a desire for intercourse with even a transitory partner. (As the clinicians report this, they imply that it is a male tendency only.) Apart from indicating that androgen is the libido hormone for both sexes, these cases suggest that androgen secretion may bear some relationship to the threshhold of arousal and to the energy with which males pursue their sexual exploits.

Experiments with monkeys have led to the conclusion that, although androgen may be significantly related to sexual behaviour, the social situation is of great importance. Female rhesus monkeys injected with androgen show an increase in the masculine practice of 'mounting', but only if they are dominant members of their group before the experiment. Among dominant females, the incidence of mounting increases from 0.8 times to 1.2 times per test (which is statistically significant) but if subordinate females are injected the incidence of mounting behaviour remains at the same low level.

So the role of sex hormones in generating signals which are relayed to the brain and converted into sexual arousal can clearly be overlaid by factors of social learning. If data did not already exist to support this contention, the cross-cultural material would supply it. Also there is a clear tendency for the sex difference in threshhold of arousal to be exaggerated quite out of proportion to its extent. Research on the general responses of males and females to visual stimuli on sexual themes shows a significant, but not enormous, sex difference. In one study, 58% of the women in the sample reported that they were sometimes sexually aroused at the sight of men, while 72% of the men reported similar reactions. 12% of the women and 54% of the men were sexually aroused by posed pictures of the opposite sex: a third of the women and three quarters of the men were excited by pictures of the sexual act. But men and women were equally excited by erotic books and films. Masters and Johnson exposed their subjects to pornographic literature, and observed a vasocongestive and clitoral reaction in 75% of the female cases, identical to that occurring in the excitement phase of sexual response. They have not so far come across a female subject who can fantasy to orgasm, although Kinsey reported that 2% of the females in his sample with a history of masturbation were able to do so, and he also reported a significant number who claimed to reach orgasm during sleep, often awakening with the violence of the orgasmic contractions.

Sex differences in the erotic content of dreams and daydreams reflect, as one might expect, differences in the sexual and social roles of male and female in our culture. Female fantasy is more often romantic and emotional than genitally sexual and erotic. Specifically sexual-erotic fantasies tend to be a male prerogative: however, during masturbation, 50% of women always have erotic fantasies, and 70% sometimes do, compared with 90% of men who say that they always do. Masturbation is to some extent an equaliser here, as it is in the amount of time required to reach orgasm.

Attempts to get statistical proof of a sex difference in fantasy have not been much of a success, but they do show how far the sex roles prescribed by society have become internalised. K M Colby took a sample of 200 males and 200 females, and noted one dream from each of them. He found a group of words and associated qualities predominating in male dreams— wife, vehicle, travel, car, and 'to hit'—and a group more characteristic of women's dreams—husband, women and 'to cry'. Like Erikson's account of sex differences in children's play, this sex difference in dream imagery faithfully reflects features of the social worlds of the sexes, including the fact that men have wives, whereas women have husbands, men travel more than women, women are allowed to cry more than men (in our culture, that is) and men are allowed and even encouraged to show more aggression than women.

Colby's attempt to extend his conclusion to the dreams of primitive tribes met with conspicuous failure. 'Wife' and 'husband' were the only two words with statistical significance. Generally, studies by anthropologists show that the kinds of fears and fantasies people have in the area of sexuality are related to their society's attitudes. Women in our society certainly have fantasies of rape, but so do men in societies where women are strong and aggressive, and this (to us) strange male fear is articulated very often in folklore (as in the Trobriander example mentioned earlier).

Another generalisation about female sexuality concerns deviation. It is held that women are less prone to sexual deviation (homosexuality, transvestism, fetishism, exhibitionism and so on) and it is assumed that this has something to do with the strength and direction of the sex drive in males and females. This in turn is usually assumed to be governed by biological factors. In actual fact, many of these deviations represent a conditioning of sexual response to specific stimuli which are usually not sexual in themselves and often become important purely by chance, through a process of association. Paul Gebhard, in discussing the role of 'situational factors in human sexual behaviour', gives an example of conditioning to what is not usually a sexual stimulus. A boy nearing puberty, but unaware of sexual arousal, became involved in a fight with a larger and more powerful girl. While struggling with her he became sexually excited for the first time, and after that he was always attracted to large, muscular, dominant females, with whom he liked to wrestle during intercourse. (At the time of Gebhard's report he was in his thirties.)

In our society this type of conditioning is more often found in males—almost exclusively so—and this has led to widespread speculation that the male's characteristic response to a wider range of stimuli than the female, and his unfortunate ability to be conditioned by irrelevant stimuli (silk stockings, black underwear, red hair, powerful women) are a function of the different roles the cerebral cortex plays in the sexual behaviour of males and females. The cerebral cortex—the outside layer of the brain, responsible for thought, memory and imagination—is

the part of the brain on which learning is heavily

dependent, and conditioning by stimuli is a kind of learning. The cortex also appears to have a direct function in sexuality, since animals can be made to perform some of their mating acts if the relevant part of their brain is electrically stimulated. This is true both of males and females, but on the other hand, male animals who have been deprived of their cortices lose the capacity for sexual behaviour (they are unable to mount and ejaculate) whereas cortexless females continue to be receptive. Not a great deal can be made of this research in its application to humans.

On the statistical incidence of sexual deviation in males and females in our society we have no reliable evidence. The law is prone to define exhibitionism (exposing the genitals) and frottery (rubbing the genitals against another person) as well as rape and homosexuality, as exclusively male offences: there are therefore no female convictions. One prominent psychiatrist declares that though females exhibit themselves in striptease shows, they never get any pleasure out of it. (In some small-scale societies, for instance the Lesu and the Kurtatchi, women do exhibit their genitals as an invitation to intercourse, and in one—the Azande—it is believed that a man will come to harm if a woman provokingly exposes her genitals to him.) Another psychiatrist puts forward the more egalitarian argument that the equivalent of the exhibited penis is not the exhibited labia, but the naked breast—and he observes that there are many social opportunities for the exhibition of the breast, which makes female exhibitionism not pathological (as it is with males) but normal. The argument acquires conviction when one considers that the breast is considered by both sexes to be as much a symbol of female sexuality as is the erect penis of male sexuality. The male concern with the size and erection potential of the penis is paralleled by the female concern over the size, shape and attractiveness of the breast: hence the bra, the bust developer, and (some at least) of the Western aversion to breast-feeding. The fact that the breast has become a specifically sexual object is connected with the

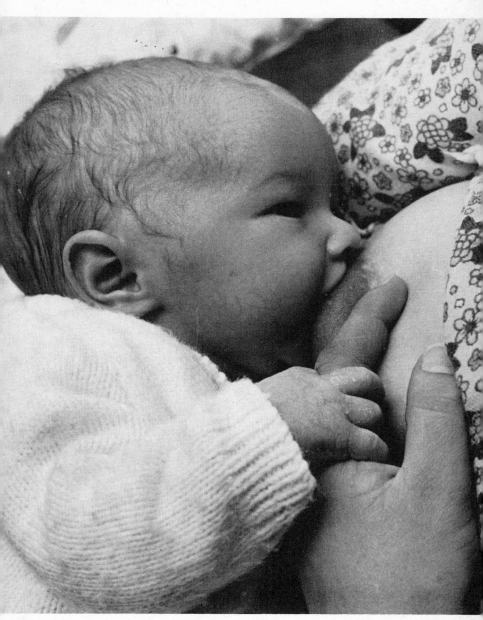

(Pictorial Press)

reluctance of women to expose their breasts to suckle a child. Their inability to accept the sexual excitement that breastfeeding often brings—a baby's sucking stimulates not only the nipple, but also contractions of the uterus—is a measure of the divorce in Western culture between femininity and sexuality (again despite the decease of the Victorians).

Sodomy and bestiality are female as well as male offences, legally speaking. Sodomy (anal intercourse) between male and female is considered to involve the consent of both of them, and intercourse with an animal is also an offence of which both sexes have been convicted. However there are few statistics and little knowledge about the sex difference in these offences.

Another deviation attributed mostly to the male has been homosexuality—erotic attraction to persons of the same sex. Kinsey's data show 4% of white males to be exclusively homosexual in erotic activity throughout their lives; the figure for females is between 1% and 3%, though 4% of his sample of *single* women were exclusively homosexual. Another sample shows 3% of all women as exclusively homosexual and 1% of married women as having some homosexual contacts. Kinsey showed 37% of white males and 13% of white females to have had some overt homosexual experience leading to orgasm between adolescence and old age. This is taken to be an index of the difference in the sexual experience of the two sexes: women are less promiscuous than men, whether they are homosexual or heterosexual in inclination.

Male homosexuality is generally reckoned to occur in about 5% of the male population. But, as D J West put it in his book on 'Homosexuality', 'Conspicuous neglect of the topic on the part of research workers, and a quite extraordinary dearth of factual information in published works, make any statement about lesbianism peculiarly hazardous.'

Referring to an earlier study made by Katharine Davis, West suggests that homosexuality among women may be characterised by a predominantly emotional rather than narrowly sexual attachment. Half of Davis's sample of 1,200 females admitted to intense emotional experiences with other women, only a quarter to physical contact. Interviews with lesbians have since confirmed the impression that the attraction between homosexual women tends to be less specifically genital-sexual than that between homosexual men.

The reason why this is so, and the reason why the incidence of lesbianism appears to be less than that of male homosexuality, may lie in both social and anatomical factors. One American psychoanalyst has observed that female homosexuals more often get married than do their male counterparts. Thus lesbianism may actually be a cause of frigidity, possibly unrecognised even in the women themselves, and the masking of lesbianism in marriage a factor explaining the apparent lesser incidence of it. Lesbians are able to get a great deal of satisfaction out of having children, and child-rearing is a female role (homosexuality is not related to lack of parental feeling in men either). Lesbians can maintain the semblance of a satisfactory marriage since they are physically capable of heterosexual intercourse even if they are unaroused in the course of it. Male homosexuals, on the other hand, have to be attracted to the point of erection before intercouse is possible, and if they can only be stimulated by other males, heterosexual intercouse is clearly ruled out.

A further reason why female homosexuality may be less likely to occur in our society is related to a contributory cause of homosexuality—identification with a person of the opposite sex. Many experts have observed that a common pattern in the childhood genesis of male homosexuality is a dominating mother and a weak or absent father. Lesbians also seem to be bound up with the parent of the opposite sex, but in a family system where the father's role is minimised by his having to spend a large part of his time away from home, male homosexuality is likely to occur more often than lesbianism, since it is the boy whose identification is in jeopardy, not the girl.

C S Ford and F A Beach, surveying patterns of sexual behaviour in 190 different societies, report that 49 of the 76 for which data is available regard homosexuality as normal. This is mostly male homosexuality but in 17 societies the reports indicate specifically female homosexuality.

Sometimes homosexuality becomes institutionalised in a culture—widely accepted and socially approved, with homosexuals occupying a distinct status. One such society is the Mohave Indians, whose attitudes towards homosexuality were described by George Devereux. The Mohave recognised two types of homosexual: male transvestites, taking the role of the woman in intercourse, and female homosexuals, taking the role of the man. These men and women seem to have been physiologically normal though, in keeping with their roles, the names given to the genital organs were reversed (the penis was called a clitoris, the testes the labia majora, the anus the vagina, and vice versa). In homosexual marriages the man-wife and woman-husband adopted all the patterns of behaviour and temperamental traits expected of normal partners. Since anal intercourse was a common practice among the Mohaves, these homosexual marriages were not deprived of a form of sexual satisfaction. Two biological females married to each other used digital immission and fake intercourse in a position enabling the vulvae to touch. Male 'wives' feigned menstruation by cutting their thighs monthly, faked pregnancy, stuffing rags to the shape of a pregnant womb, and imitated labour. Female 'husbands' were socially recognised to be the fathers of their wives' children.

Devereux gives no data on the incidence of male and female homosexuality. However, it is unlikely that a society would have reached such a high degree of institutionalisation in creating two social roles for people whose sexual identity conflicted with their biological sex, if there had not been a number of people taking up the roles involved. Devereux's account, like those of many anthropologists studying the phenomenon of homosexuality in other cultures, is heavily biased towards the male, with an underlying assumption that because female homosexuality appears to be less common than male in our society, it will be so in others.

Some observers have seen a relationship between personality type and the expression of sexuality which holds true for males as well as females (as does the relationship between intellectual achievement and personality noted in the previous chapter). L M Terman reported in 1957 that the relationship between certain personality traits and the capacity for orgasm in a sample of women reached statistical significance. Women with a low capacity for orgasm were less confident and less sure of themselves, more emotionally unstable and sensitive, and more conformist in their attitude towards authority and convention. These same personality traits are found more often in males who are less self-assertive sexually and have more sexual problems generally (perhaps to do with impotence or the fear of it) than in males whose approach to sex is the more usually dominant and straightforward one. Other researchers (notably A H Maslow) have subsequently reported that 'dominant' women appear to enjoy sex more (like the Trobrianders). One might also add the speculation that because more females than males in our society exhibit 'passive' traits, more of them find it hard to enjoy sex and have difficulty in reaching orgasm.

A final area in which explanations of male-female differences in sexuality have been sought is psychology—particularly Freudian psychology. According to this school of thought, the evolution of male and female personality, and the development of sexuality, are both part of the same process. Compared to the factors already discussed, psycho-analytic theory does little to explain why male and female sexuality appear to differ; however, the coherence between the Freudian view of sexuality and the Freudian explanation of personality formation has been very influential, and a brief account of these theories will suggest some of the points at which psychoanalysis has raised a cultural sex difference to the status of a universal and natural distinction.

In traditional psychoanalytic theory, three basic features determine the different development of sexuality in males and females: the exteriority of the male genitals, the female's destiny of motherhood, and the structure of the family.

Both boys and girls are said to pass through the oral and anal stages in early infancy: then both become more specifically sexual in their interests. The penis becomes an object of attention to the boy and her clitoris to the girl, but at this point male and female sexuality take diverging paths. The female child is disappointed in her clitoris, wishing it to be more male in size and function; she turns away from her mother (whom she holds responsible) and projects her love towards her father. From her father she hopes to get a penis: later, when it is clear she will not, she translates this desire into the desire to bear a child. The male, however, around his third year, becomes intensely and sexually attracted to his mother, a passion which he gives up a year or so later because of the fear that his father might take revenge on him by castration. The sexuality of both sexes then passes into a stage of latency, re-emerging near puberty in recognisably masculine and feminine forms.

The penis envy from which the female child suffers, and the way she later equates the penis with a child, give rise to the traits of passivity, masochism and narcissism that make up the female character. Passivity, for example, comes from her abandonment of clitoral stimulation and from the onset of the maternal urge during the period of intense attachment to the father. Partly because of these qualities the female sex drive is said to be much weaker than the male's. Feminine personality and sexuality are both therefore a response—a solution—which the female child devises to the problems of penis envy. Before her discovery of the missing penis, she is 'masculine' in character—that is, she shares the same interests, genital and nongenital, as boys. After her sight of the male organ she acquires femininity almost as a compensation. (At this point things may go wrong and she may become either neurotic or masculine.) Because of these compensatory masochistic, narcissistic and passive qualities, her sex drive and her general libidinous energy are much weaker than in the male. But she has a heightened inner emotional life and a capacity to give maternal tenderness not only to her children but to her male partner. This tenderness cannot coexist with genital sexual excitement, localised and orgiastic as the male's is: in any case the reproductive purpose is achieved without any activity on the part of the female in intercourse. What the normal woman experiences in intercourse is not pleasure but a kind of masochistic pain. The sexual life cannot be divorced from motherhood—both the reality of it and the desire for it. The simple desire to rid oneself of sexual tension which characterises adult male sexuality is missing in the female, whose sexuality is bound up in a complex manner with the development of femininity, and particularly with the evolution of a specifically maternal emotion.

Psychoanalysis tends to regard sexuality itself as male, as it does 'libido', the concept of motivating energy responsible in humans for both sexual and non-sexual achievements. A basic weakness in the whole of this approach is, as Kate Millett has observed, its male bias. Freud and his followers built up a theory of feminine sexuality to account for the differences they observed between the sexes in their own sexually repressed and male-dominated society. A host of unsupportable assumptions prop up this theory of sexuality in females: the assumption that a female child believes herself to be anatomically inferior to the male (or believes the male to be superior); the assumption that while females envy males their penises, males do not envy females their wombs and their maternity; the assumption that the female child blames her mother (and not her father) for failing to provide her with a penis, and so on. Hence psychoanalytic theory is open to attack on many grounds. Not only was Freudian theory developed within the framework of a patriarchal family system; it fits only a culture in which masculinity and femininity are defined in particular ways. Freud's insistence on the discovery of the missing penis could hardly withstand the realities of preliterate societies where nakedness is the rule; nor is penis envy likely in cultures where little girls are told how lucky they are to have wombs and so to be able to become mothers, and where the male role is consistently devalued. Bruno Bettelheim has described many of the rituals in such societies, which eloquently express the male desire to emulate the achievements of women. The evidence from anthropology shows that the development of sexuality in males and females alike is responsive to a range of social values and rules which govern its legitimate expression, rather than to the biologically constant genital ground-plan of their bodies. Furthermore, penis envy and womb envy may be so named for their symbolic meaning only, and the actual envy men and women have of each other may not be of their genitals and reproductive organs but of their social prestige and economic function. In Freud's time, the feminine role was of low social value, and few women achieved anything of socially recognised value outside the province of home and family.

Differences in the sexuality of male and female have been variously attributed to differences in (a) their anatomies (b) the functioning of their hormones (c) their psychologies (d) their personalities and (e) the cultural learning processes to which they are subjected.

Of these five, only the first two and the last are contrasting explanations, since the psychology and personality of male and female largely depend on culture. In fact the role of anatomy in determining sexuality must remain a purely hypothetical one until some explanation is given on how the two connect. As it stands the statement 'anatomy is destiny' offers no real explanation. Freudian theory can be interpreted as a massive attempt to take on the one hand distinctions of anatomy and on the other distinctions of 'destiny' (or social role) and propose a series of processes by which one might lead to the other. One example of this is the genesis of penis envy for which the Freudian 'explanation' is the little girl's sighting of the male genital and her subsequent envy of men. While these indubitably occur—some little girls do see penises and women do envy men—nothing may follow from the first other than a mere recognition of the anatomical sex difference, while the second may arise not from the first, but instead from an entirely realistic perception of the male's social roles as superior in power, prestige and interest.

In industrial cultures (and in some others too) the sexual relationship between male and female has been subsumed in the general power relationship of the sexes. This—the thesis of Kate Millett's 'Sexual Politics'—has far-reaching implications for many areas of sex differentiation, including sexuality itself.

A culture which allots political and economic power to the male and gives him the prestige of playing the public roles, invites a number of responses from the female, to whom these rights and responsibilities are denied. One response is rebellion, epitomised in the emancipation movement of the late nineteenth and early twentieth centuries, and now in the women's liberation movement. But the demand for liberation and the techniques of rebellion are only possible for women who are conscious of rights denied and of the patriarchal bias that history has built into our culture. For the others, one possible response is to compensate for lack of power by obtaining a vicarious emotional satisfaction from exercising control over the powerful (blackmail is one form of this).

Unfortunately, a woman who responds in this way distorts her own personality. She uses her sexuality as a means of attracting males, which is necessary since the 'possession' of a male is the only means to power, and since she must have a male to support her if she wishes to bear children (and this wish is the only distinctive part of female sexuality as defined by a patriarchal culture). This use of her sexuality as a means of keeping a male means that she must subordinate her own female desires and needs to those of the male. Inevitably all this distorts the female's own self-image, so that she sees herself as secondary, inferior, weak and placatory, and as relying on her sexual charms for a multitude of purposes, including the central one of economic survival.

This distinctively female use of sexuality lies behind the finding that dominant women enjoy sex more than submissive ones. Submissive women are unable to assert themselves sexually and are therefore able to enjoy only one kind of satisfaction, that which is wholly dependent on the technical expertise of the male. They cannot tell their lovers even what they want done to their own bodies, and the awareness of this acts as a barrier to the physical sensation of the experience itself. 'Dominant' women on the other hand are not afraid of their sexual aggression, do not interpret it as pseudomasculinity (except in the sense that the norm of sexuality is male, as all norms tend to be male in a male-oriented culture) and are not repulsed by the physical needs and sensations of their own bodies.

Some progressive psychiatric thought is now taking account of the fact that this long conditioning of the female to a particular kind of sexual response (or lack of response) is a facet of the maleness of our culture, and this is leading to the conclusion that some of the so-called sex differences in sexuality are due to conditioning and learning, rather than to innate and pre-cultural factors. The cross-cultural data support this; so does the material quoted earlier in this chapter, showing that the sexual responses of the two sexes are largely determined by their different sexual experiences, which in turn are determined by their cultural roles. So also does the recent biological material, and this is of particular value in helping to finally quash the debate about the vaginal versus the clitoral orgasm. To show that the ultimate sexual response, the orgasm, is physiologically identical in male and female, except for the minor necessary difference of organ and secretion, is a landmark of great importance in the study of human sexuality.

For the study of female sexuality in particular, generalisations from the animal world have been influential and extremely depressing. The infrahuman female primate, says the expert, does not have an orgasm—conclusion, the human female does not have or need an orgasm either? The chimpanzee, on the other hand, does appear to masturbate, which perhaps should cheer feminists up a little. Also, female chimpanzees often take the initiative in sexual liasons, and so do not confirm the conventional idea of the passivity of the female.

The analogy becomes increasingly ridiculous when we add that the nonhuman female primate has no hymen, menopause, artificial feeding bottle, or voluntary relief from procreation. The males of these species are dominant, aggressive, and sexually assertive, and show no desire or ability to give the female pleasure. This is equally absurd in its application to human culture, enabling the patriarchal world to be supported in its very foundations, justifying the aggressive acts of the male in the bedroom by reference to the jungle, and providing a rationale for aggressive acts in the distinctly human world of social, economic, and political affairs.

To study the evolution of sex differences in sexuality one can, of course, study the chimpanzee, and speculate on the origins of the female orgasm. Is it an evolving trait which is not yet fully established, itself a product of culture? Or is it a 'regressive' development, a distinctly human invention which is to be deplored for its tendency to distract females from the central business of maternity? Whatever the answer—and it is doubtful whether we will ever know it—it is surely much more important to study the whole moulding of personality and sexual response by culture, and in different forms of *human* society.

5

Sex and social role

It is often said that the division of labour by sex is a universal characteristic of human societies. What kind of evidence is produced to support this statement?

Professor George Murdock has surveyed the data for 224 societies (mostly preliterate) and shows that the tendency to segregate economic activities in one way or another according to sex is strong. Taking a list of 46 different activities, he suggests that some are more often masculine than feminine, and vice versa. For example, lumbering is an exclusively masculine activity in 104 of his societies and exclusively feminine in 6: cooking is exclusively feminine in 158 and exclusively masculine in 5. Hunting, fishing, weapon making, boat building and mining tend to be masculine, while grinding grain and carrying water tend to be feminine. Activities that are less consistently allotted to one sex include preparing the soil, planting, tending and harvesting the crops, 'burden bearing' and body mutilation.

The conclusion that can be drawn from Murdock's survey is that every society does have rules about which activities are suitable for males and which for females; but these rules vary a great deal from one society to another, and generalisations about how biology inevitably dictates their form and content are not supported by the data.

However, one must look further than Murdock's sample for a confirmation of this: his collection of 224 societies represents a mere fragment of the 5,000 or so distinctly separate cultures known to exist or to have existed, or even of the 2,000 for which we have adequate ethnographic data. There are many difficulties in using the data to produce the sort of statistics that Murdock claims to have found. The anthropologist Evans-Pritchard has listed as problems of this method (to which Murdock's work is prone) 'poor sampling, crude itemisation, arbitrary and inadequate criteria of classification,' and (in Murdock's own case) 'an almost unbelievably uncritical use of sources'.

In 'Women and Men', one of the earlier books on sex differences, Amram Scheinfeld proposed a theory

Balinese women pounding rice   (Paul Popper)

of the origins of the division of labour between male and female (the division which Murdock believes his data confirm):

there are no Adam + Eve situations there is always soc

> Let us go back to Adam and Eve. In the very beginning they may have started out to do the same tasks. But presently there was a child on the way, and as Eve's movements began to be slowed up, the heavier tasks were no longer possible for her. To Adam, then, fell largely the jobs of fighting off dangerous beasts, killing and bringing in big game, moving heavy rocks, etc. When her child was born, Eve had to nurse it, and her movements continued to be impeded and limited, and by the time the first baby was weaned, there was probably another coming along. So regardless of how equally Adam and Eve might have started out to do the same kind of jobs, they would have fallen into more or less divergent patterns of activity. ❯

of course! "origins"! of

This type of explanation obviously applies far more to small-scale preliterate societies than to large-scale, literate, technologically developed ones. Nevertheless it is used to explain and justify the differences that persist in modern industrial societies, in most of which the majority of mothers of small children have no other role than the domestic one. A UNESCO survey in the 1960s of 'Images of Women in Society' revealed a virtually universal opposition to the employment of mothers when their children are young. In all the countries studied (which included Poland, France, Canada, Morocco, and Austria) neglect of children and household duties were given as reasons for the opposition to maternal employment, and almost everywhere popular opinion believed that different occupations were proper to the two sexes, with the woman's role centred on the home.

Both contemporary beliefs about the economic division of labour by sex, and the opinions about its origins held by Scheinfeld and shared by many others, contain a number of assumptions about the connection between reproductive and economic tasks.

The first assumption is that the responsibilities of motherhood (pregnancy, breastfeeding, daily attention to the child's needs over a period of years) mean that she must give up other work.

The second assumption is that maternity is a relatively sedentary occupation requiring relatively low levels of energy and strength.

The third is that the same is true of domestic work in general.

The fourth is that in traditional preliterate small-scale societies (like the one Adam and Eve hypothetically established) women are confined to domestic occupations which are marginal to the society's main economic tasks.

The fifth is that the female does not have the physical strength and energy of the male, and therefore cannot share in such jobs as tree-felling and hunting.

These assumptions prop up the argument for the functional necessity of sex differences in social role—the argument that human society requires a division of labour by sex as a condition of survival. Without them the argument collapses. This chapter is devoted mainly to considering the truth of these assumptions, and questioning their relevance to generalisations about the influence of sex on social role.

What generalisations can be made about the rules for allocating tasks and roles by sex? And what rules are made in practice by differing societies, including our own? As each assumption is taken in turn, the appearance of biological necessity comes to seem more mythical than real. Certain myths held in Western culture about its own sophisticated and democratic methods for allocating roles by sex also lose some of their acceptability.

In the first assumption, motherhood is seen as leading to necessary differences in the kind of economic roles the sexes can perform. There is not actually much substance to this. Most small-scale societies do not ban physical exertion during

131

pregnancy, lactation, or in the early years of motherhood generally. Whatever work it is customary for women to do is continued into pregnancy. Colin Turnbull describes childbirth among the Mbuti pygmies:

❛ The mother is likely to be off on the hunt or on the trail somewhere when birth takes place: there is no lessening of activity for her during pregnancy. Childbirth is said to be effected easily, with complications only rarely happening...Within two hours of delivery if birth took place in the camp, the mother is apt to appear in the doorway of her hut, with a bundle wrapped in bark cloth held in her arms. Within the same period of time, if birth took place on the trail, she will continue her journey. ❜

In many societies women continue with their usual agricultural and domestic work until the moment of delivery: the Bamenda women studied by Phyllis Kaberry work at their farms (often several miles from their homes) until birth is imminent. After giving birth, they rest for about three weeks and then return to normal work. Women in Alor, who also work throughout pregnancy, return to the fields and gardens after a break of ten days following childbirth. Yahgan women of Tierra del Fuego have a rest period of between fifteen minutes and one day following childbirth. Thereafter they gather shellfish, lift loads and engage in rowing as though nothing had happened. Sometimes pregnancy is even considered a reason for extra activity. The Tubatulabel woman believes that if she stays in her house during her pregnancy she will get fat and the baby will not move; so she works hard and climbs mountains. The Ainu women of Japan exercise hard during pregnancy to keep the foetus small and encourage swift labour. Activity during labour is often prescribed for the same reason—in one nomadic Saharan tribe pregnant women walk up and down hills during labour, only returning to the tent for delivery.

132   The tie of lactation between mother and child,

although extremely restricting in modern society, is not so in traditional small-scale social groups. Many preliterate peoples have institutionalised the practice of communal breast-feeding, according to which each child is regularly fed by a number of different women. This frees the individual woman from the need to remain in or around the home for the period that her child is fed on human milk (commonly two or three years). Margaret Mead reports that in Samoa children are frequently suckled by other women of the household, and become used to a number of mothers. Among the Dakota, sisters share the breastfeeding of all their children between them. Often a small child does not come home for several days at a time: 'He's over at his mother's' says his (biological) mother. Here the meaning of the word 'mother' is not biological relatedness, but the milk tie, which is diffused in a series of relationships.

The Alor also practice communal breastfeeding within the kin group. Every child has access to many breasts, and the mother's are no more consistently available—because of her other duties—than those of other women. After the rest period which follows childbirth, babies are left in the villages while the mothers work. Bamenda women leave babies older than three months in the villages, feeding them only morning and night. Bororo women consider themselves more or less equally available to all the unweaned children of the group; Arunta women nurse each other's children and are said to argue regularly about which of them shall stay in the camp to do it and which shall go out after food.

Of the two elements in motherhood, the biological and the social, modern society emphasises the latter most strongly, insisting that the social relationship between mother and child established in the first years of life is the foundation of adult security and mental health. There is therefore a strong tendency to insist that motherhood acts as a bar to economic activity because of the child's needs. No such emphasis is found in small-scale societies, and it is hardly likely to have restricted Adam and Eve in their choice of sex-appropriate economic tasks. Modern medicine and psychiatry provide no data to support the contention that children need their mothers, though there is incontrovertible evidence that children need good physical care, stable emotional relationships, and a certain minimum of verbal and nonverbal stimulation if they are to achieve their human potential. One reason for the importance of motherhood in the modern industrialised world is that children are dependent for much longer than they are in small-scale societies. Dependence goes hand in hand with economic liability, and this dual fact makes the attendance of adult upon child a real necessity.

But *female* attendance? Parenthood consists of both motherhood and fatherhood; the fact that industrialised societies tend to play down the role of the father does not make this a universal human necessity. Motherhood may restrict the social and economic roles of women—but so may fatherhood restrict the roles of men. Other societies exist in which men and women share more or less equally in the tasks arising out of pregnancy and labour (in some they are even thought to share the physiological processes).

The Arapesh, for example, consider that the business of bearing and rearing a child belongs to father and mother equally, and equally disqualifies them for other roles. Men as well as women 'make' and 'have' babies, and the verb 'to bear a child' is used indiscriminately of either a man or a woman. Child-bearing is believed to be as debilitating for the man as it is for the woman. The father goes to bed and is described as 'having a baby' when the child is born. The same dietary and other restrictions that apply to the newly delivered mother apply to the father too, and he, like the mother, has to be ritually purified. Neither parent is allowed sexual intercourse (with the other or with anyone else) till the child is a year old. The father shares all the routine activities of child care as naturally as the mother. Both parents have other duties: for the male,

134

housebuilding, sewing thatch, clearing and fencing land, carving, growing yams; for the female, cooking, fetching firewood and water, weeding and carrying. Whichever parent has the more pressing duties hands the child over to the other, and neither is regarded as a substitute for the other but as engaged in the shared joy and responsibility of 'growing children'.

It is common to find restrictions imposed on prospective fathers. Some of them may be without rational foundation, but they are none the less binding. Often husbands are forbidden to go to war or to hunt during their wives' pregnancies. The Arunta husband, for example, does not use the boomerang or spear to kill large game while his wife is pregnant. The prospective Malekulan father does not leave the house as the birth of his child approaches. The Hopi forbid the father to injure any living creature in any way: husbands in Ifugao cannot hunt, kill or cut anything during the nine months of pregnancy, and relatives even have to cut wood for them, though they are allowed to bundle it and carry it home. The reasoning behind these prohibitions, which is explicit in some societies, is that any aggressive act by the prospective father or mother may harm the unborn baby.

In the same way, an emphasis on the social (rather than medical) importance of fatherhood to the child may restrict a man's other activities, just as the stress placed on motherhood in modern industrialised societies restricts the woman.

The day-by-day care of young children, which falls to the Arapesh father as a matter of course, is a normal occupation for men in a number of societies. The Trobriand Islanders are renowned for their ignorance of the father's biological role in repro- duction, but they stress the need for the father to share with the mother all the tasks involved in bringing up chidren. Whether the social father is actually the child's biological father or not, he shares fully in its care: he fondles and and carries the baby and holds it on his knees,a task which is his special prerogative rather than the mother's. He cleans it

135

when it soils itself, and gives it mashed vegetable food almost from birth. Malinowski observed the same sort of paternal behaviour among the Australian aboriginies. If a child's father dies before it is born, it is put to death by the mother, because the father is so necessary to the child that life is incompatible with his absence. (The Eskimos of Greenland kill a baby if its mother dies in childbirth for the same reason: among the Eskimos the domestic divison of labour is much closer to that of modern industrialised society, with mothers almost totally responsible for the daily rearing of their children.)

These cultural variations on the theme of parenthood can only be considered 'deviant' and 'abnormal' if we assume that because we in our society do things a certain way, this must be the best or only way of doing them. In actual fact, putting child care in the hands of women alone is not necessarily the best way of doing things, nor the most natural, nor should we think of it as a rule which holds in all but a few insignificant and peculiar cultures. In fact, we have some strictly non-rational beliefs of our own about the ways in which sex, and particularly reproduction, determines the gender roles of male and female.

For example, the dangerous effect of heavy work on mother and child, during pregnancy and before, is usually put forward as the reason why women should not exert themselves physically beyond a certain point. Actually the fact that many other societies do not follow this rule confirms the recent conclusion experts in undustrialised societies have come to that the medical data do not support the belief that work is likely to cause problems in pregnancy and childbirth. The real relationship between heavy work before pregnancy and the incidence of miscarriages, still births, etc, is a very indirect one, due to the probability that women from poor homes with inadequate nutrition will both engage in heavy work and be likely to miscarry: what causes the failure is not the work but the poor nutrition in childhood. Despite a great deal of research, there is no systematic

136

and conclusive evidence relating infant deaths just before or just after birth with the mother's activity during pregnancy. There is a relationship between work during pregnancy and low birth-weight, but it is a spurious one: both low birth-weight and work during pregnancy are associated with a battery of other factors including socio-economic status, maternal height and age, prenuptial conception, housing conditions, and level of antenatal care. There are no studies on the relationship between physical exertion and the outcome of pregnancy in societies outside the industrialised West but there is some evidence that physical exercise promotes an easy labour and hence a healthy infant both in our own and in other, dissimilar, cultures—confirming the views of those primitive women who believe in work rather than rest as a preparation for childbirth.

So much, then, for the first of the assumptions that are used to justify the economic division of labour by sex. The second and third assumptions— that maternity and domesticity are occupations requiring low levels of activity and energy—are to some extent fictions also. It is doubtful whether maternity is a passive and sedentary occupation in any society, and the assumption that it is so is based more on the status of motherhood (as an unpaid, traditionally female occupation) in modern industrial society than on any realistic evaluation of what it actually involves. As all mothers (and some fathers) know, child care is physically exhausting and mentally demanding work: it needs tireless vigilance, a great deal of energy, and a kind of protectiveness and responsibility that is aggressive rather than passive, implying as it does the ability to stand up for the child and fight for its rights in a world that is not always sympathetic. In particular, the physical strength needed in child care is by no means negligible. A child aged one year may weigh well over twenty pounds and a child of two, who may still need to be carried or physically restrained for much of the time, may easily weigh thirty pounds.

In the same way, the energy demanded by

domestic work has been conventionally underrated. It seems sedentary and light to those who not only view it with disdain, but who see it from a mechanised perspective where washing-machines, electric ovens and so forth have taken the 'burden' out of it. Traditionally domestic work has required—and in unmechanised cultures continues to require—considerable physical stamina and ability to carry loads, to name but two qualities. For instance, water carrying, where the domestic water supply is some distance from the home, as it often is, needs as much energy as, say, cutting down trees. The preparation of food is also often exhausting and time-consuming. Phyllis Kaberry, in her study of Bamenda women, refers to it as 'the last straw to break a woman's back after a long day's work on the farm and a weary trudge home.' Kaberry describes the daily work involved in the preparation of grain porridge, the main food among the Bamenda and in other parts of Africa:

❛ The maize is rubbed off the cob by hand, pounded in a mortar for a few minutes, and then winnowed in the grindstone, which is usually placed in the rear of the hut, is some 24 inches long and 16-20 inches broad. A woman kneels at one end, places a slightly concave basket at the other to catch the flour, grasps a small tortoise shaped stone with both hands and then grinds. On such occasions when I timed the process it took about one hour for three pounds of grain. Generally one grinding is considered sufficient [for a day] unless there is a sickly child or a feast. ❜

In the light of all this, the idea that the males do the 'heavy' work while the females are occupied with 'light' domestic tasks seems to be a merely fictional opposition between two forms of work which both demand energy and strength. (Indeed Murdock's own tabulation of the division of labour by sex shows 'burden bearing' to be a predominantly female activity.)

138   √   Many societies put child-care among the occupa-

tions carrying high status rather than low, reversing the 'civilised' practise. An inquiry as to why people in Bamenda mourn four days for a woman, while only three for a man, drew the explanation (which was given by the men) 'A woman is the one who bears the people...Women are very important. Women are like God, because they bear children.' They go on to say: 'What work can a man do? A woman bears a child, then takes a hoe, goes to the field, and is working there...A man only buys palm oil. Men only build houses.'

These comments reveal the flaws in the fourth assumption, that the main work of women through-out history and across cultures has been domestic, and therefore marginal as a contribution to the economic welfare of society. Perhaps the most important of all the reasons why the division of labour between the sexes is not universally con-structed around the polarity of sedentary female and active male is the fact that the traditional female role over wide areas of the world has involved women in economically productive work outside the home. This is contrary to the modern belief that the employment of women outside the home is a twentieth-century phenomenon, possible only in industrialised societies where the state takes over some of the maternal role in child care and education. In 'The Family Among the Australian Aborigines' Malinowski wrote:

> ❛ A very important point is that the woman's share in labour was of much more *vital importance* to the maintenance of the household than man's work...even the food supply, contributed by the women, was far more important than the man's share...food collected by women was the staple food of the natives... economically [the family] is entirely dependent upon woman's work. ❜

Among the Australian aborigines women collect vegetable food, dig for roots and hunt small animals (leaving men the sporadic task of catching large animals). In other areas their traditional role has been

A Kikuyu woman carries her load of wood while her daughter
trudges behind with a lighter load on her head. (Paul Popper)

to cultivate the land. This has been a particularly strong tradition over much of Africa (though it is also found elsewhere, for instance in Thailand and Cambodia). In Africa women have been the chief, if not sole, cultivators of the land for centuries. The male role (at least before the European conquest) was felling trees—a task mostly performed by fifteen- to eighteen-year-old boys—and also hunting and warfare. With the decline of the last two roles, men became very largely unemployed. Methodical studies of women's role in agriculture undertaken between 1940 and 1962 show that even at this late date women did between 60% and 80% of the total agricultural work in a sample of African peoples, living in Senegal, Gambia, Nigeria, Uganda, and Kenya.

In the African community described by Kaberry, the women farm all available arable land. Because of the complex system of inheritance, the land farmed by each woman tends to be divided into plots and widely scattered over her husband's and her mother's villages. Out of a sample of twenty-one women, the average number of plots per woman was eight. One of these women, a mother aged thirty-five with five dependants, worked fourteen plots, covering 1.8 acres. Of these, nine plots were within ten minutes walk of the compound, two were within thirty minutes, two an hour away, and one very large one was ninety minutes away over two steep hills, one of which rose 1,200 feet from the valley floor. Women here spend about two thirds of the year farming, and the remaining third on other activities within the compound, including pottery making. Men, on the other hand, spend about ten days a year on agricultural work. They may help women to collect firewood (which takes an hour or so each day) but they spend most of their time in crafts and other activities that bring in a cash income, by working at home or in the market place. With this cash income they buy certain household products—salt, oil, meat, fish—and save for marriage payments. That they work far less hard than the women is indicated by the number of recreation clubs they belong to, and the

141

number of afternoons they spend drinking wine and 'arranging financial aid'. While the normal routine for a woman's day begins at dawn, when she goes off to the farms (having already roused and fed her children) the men loiter in the compound, do a little desultory sweeping, gossip, complete their toilet, and go off to visit their friends.

In such societies, the division of labour between the sexes seems to place the main burden on female shoulders. Malinowski commented on this:

❛ It is easy to see that the amount of work allotted to women is *considerably greater* and that their labour is much *harder* than men's work...It appears that the sexual division of labour is based only partly on differences in the natural capacities of the sexes. Heavier work ought naturally to be performed by men; here the contrary obtains. Only so far as the hunting is allotted to men and collecting to women, do natural gifts appear to be taken into account. But even here, the women's work appears to be much more exacting, inasmuch as it requires a steady strain, patience and regularity. ❜

The heritage of this tradition, in which women are indispensable as productive members of society, is evident in present-day African society. In many places a woman who has no craft or trade and is wholly dependent on her husband is regarded with contempt. In Yoruba society, a girl's upbringing is calculated to give her a means of earning her livelihood, without which she is not fit to marry. Many women are traders: in the 1960 census of Nigeria 77% of the working women described themselves as traders—and they controlled 66% of the country's trade. A woman's trade is very important to her and often gets more attention than her home, since she may be away from home for weeks and months at a time buying and selling. (At these times she leaves her children in the communal care of the village.) Even in the Muslim areas of Africa women are expected to trade. In Zaria, Northern Nigeria, women are responsible for their daughters' dowries, make their own contribution to their sons' marriage payments, and provide their own cooking utensils, the children's clothes, and their own ornaments. Some men may be financially dependent on their wives, and this is considered no disgrace.

The fifth and final assumption, which takes the inequality of male and female in physical strength and energy as a reason for the division between them, also distorts the evidence. The reason why women do not catch large fish or hunt large animals as often as they gather crops or look for firewood, is, according to this argument, due to the greater suitability of the male physique for these tasks. Actually, of course, the distinction between males and females in size and strength varies between cultural groups (as we saw in Chapter 1) and also between individuals irrespective of sex. Secondly, the greater musculature of the male which is responsible for his superior strength is developed by heavy work. In Bali, where males do little heavy work, males and females resemble each other in body size and shape. But Balinese men who work as dock coolies under European supervision develop the heavy musculature we think of as a male characteristic. Hence the greater strength of the male is at least partly a result of the fact that he exerts himself more, and in cultures where this is not the tradition there may hence be much less difference between men and women. Where males customarily fell trees and hunt large animals, they develop the appropriate habits of body and mind; and where women carry water and pound grain they are likely to be conditioned in ways that produce the character- istic patterns of physical strength and energy those tasks demand. Individuals of one sex can in fact cultivate the other sex's pattern of physical activity— as was demonstrated, for instance, in Western societies during the Second World War, when women took over many of the mens' jobs, including some that involved heavy work and mechanical skill.

Hunting and fighting are shown in Murdock's tabulation to be masculine activities, but the many

English women at work in the second world war (Fox Photos)

instances (found in both small-scale and industrialised societies) of women hunting and fighting show how flexible the allocation of sex roles can be.

(?) [handwritten]

Women are reported as taking part in fighting among the Nambikwara, the Eskimo, Indian tribes of the Upper Missouri, Indian tribes of British Columbia, the Mohave Indians, the Cocopa, the Mbuti pygmies, and various Albanian tribes. Among the Nambikwara (a technologically primitive people living in the Brazilian interior described by Lévi-Strauss) some women regularly hunt and go warring with their husbands. It is their duty to collect the main food supply, and this involves not only digging up roots and collecting crops but killing animals. (As wives in polygamous marriages they are exempted from the usual duties of domesticity, and only the first wife has to look after the home and the children.)

this is unusual, tho... [handwritten]

The legendary Amazons, thought to be a South American tribe but actually a West African people living in the ancient kingdom of Dahomey, boasted the military use of women on a vast scale. Amazons were women recruited by the king as members of his regular army. In 1845 it was estimated that, out of an army of twelve thousand, five thousand were women. They were armed with blunderbusses, muskets, and knives with eighteen-inch blades, and by every report they fought like men and with equal energy and success. An English commentator, writing in 1893, suggested that the introduction of a similar practice into England would solve the problem of 'old maids'.

or lack... [handwritten] *(?)* [handwritten]

In our own time, women have been, and are, active fighters. In the 1941 Yugoslav Liberation war, for instance, around 100,000 women carried arms as active fighters: 25,000 were killed in action, 40,000 were wounded, and 3,000 became disabled, pensionable veterans.

In some of these societies, the woman's fighting role has been compatible with marriage and motherhood: in others it has not. An Amazon soldier who took a lover was executed, together with her lover, in what missionaries described as a 'horrible manner'; but the female Nambikwara warrior is by definition a married one, and the Mbuti woman who hunts does so irrespective of marriage, pregnancy or lactation. Similarly, men have sometimes been debarred from hunting and war by their other social roles, and fatherhood has been a prime disqualifier.

How then do we explain the patterning of the sexual division of labour in particular societies? We can do so best in terms of beliefs about masculinity and femininity and beliefs about maternity and paternity.

When the father of an unborn child is prohibited from aggressive activity during gestation it is because of a belief about the alliance between father and child—about the nature of fatherhood. In societies where it is thought proper for a pregnant woman to lift heavy hundles of wood, it is, similarly, a belief about the feminine role that is responsible, a deeply rooted attitude to the state of prospective mother-hood as natural, active, aggressive and healthy. Both the similarities and the variations in the ways different societies allocate tasks to men and women can be convincingly explained in terms of the system of beliefs prevailing in each society. As Murdock has said:

It is unnecessary to invoke innate psychological differences to account for the division of labour by sex; the indisputable differences in reproductive functions suffice to lay out the broad lines of cleavage. New tasks as they arise are assigned to one sphere of activities or the other in accordance with convenience and precedent.

'Convenience' and 'precedent' are matters of culture, evolving without any necessary reference to biology. Since the reproductive distinction between male and female is the one universal, societies use it as a basis for allotting other tasks. The biological specialisation suggests other specialisations, but the actual pattern of male and female activities will be devised by each society according to its beliefs about the reproductive functions of men and women, and these beliefs are culturally determined.

The degree to which they can vary from one society to another has led Margaret Mead, in discussing the cross-cultural significance of John Bowlby's work on the mother-child tie, to conclude: 'Primitive materials, therefore, give no support to the theory that there is a "natural" connexion between conditions of human gestation and delivery and appropriate cultural practices.'

Despite the differences, then, in the ways different societies allocate work between the sexes, the use of sex as a criterion seems to be a feature of most, if not all, societies. The anthropologist Claude Lévi-Strauss considers that some form of the sexual division of labour (as he calls it) is a device which establishes the mutual dependency of the sexes upon one another, and hence is probably the prerequisite of marriage. Speculations along these lines about the reasons for the division of labour by sex have produced in their time some very ingenious, but unhappily false, ideas, like Durkheim's statement that in very primitive societies both the sexual division of labour and the solidarity of marriage are rudimentary. Lévi-Strauss himself has shown how the idea of marriage and the family as a unit can be very influential in the lives of a very simple people (the Nambikwara) lacking almost any elaborate culture.

The degree of differentiation between male and female roles varies within a wide range. Sometimes the rules are merely preferential, and very little anxiety is shown by either sex over temporary reversals of the rule. Cora du Bois reports that in Alor, although there are distinctions between the economic roles of the sexes, it is not thought unhealthy for anyone to take on the other sex's work—rather they are admired for possessing a supplementary skill. The women control the subsistence economy and the men occupy themselves with financial deals (like the men of Bamenda, they have no basic economic role) but many men are passionate horticulturalists and many women have financial skills. In some cultures, on the other hand,

These young men of the Abelam tribe in New Guinea are
dressed as 'wives' in a ritual parade.   (Anthony Forge)

where horticulture is defined as a female pursuit, a proclivity for it in a man is regarded as proof of sexual deviation. In yet others, a special category may even be created for females who excel in pursuits assigned to both sexes.

The Mbuti pygmies described by Colin Turnbull in 'Wayward Servants' have a social structure in which the function of biological sex as a determinant of social role and status seems to be negligible. Hunting and gathering are the main activities on which they depend for survival, and both sexes take part. They also share political decisions and have the same social status. There is very little division of labour by sex; men often care for even the youngest children. Pregnancy is no bar to hunting, though in the neighbouring cultural area there is a taboo, to which the Mbuti pay lip service, on pregnant and menstruating women *and their husbands* taking part in the hunt. The Mbuti language distinguishes between the sexes only in terms of parenthood: they have words for 'mother' and 'father' but not for 'girl' and 'boy', 'woman' and 'man'. Where other societies, in their rituals, emphasize the distinctions between the sexes, Mbuti rituals emphasize the lack of them, and this does not seem to give rise to any anxiety about sex roles.

The Mbuti represent one extreme. At the other are those societies which impose rigid sex roles, and in which this may give rise to great anxiety. The Mundurucu Indians of central Brazil are an example of a society in which the polarisation of sex roles and sex groupings has become a primary structural element. The physical and social separation of the sexes is virtually complete: men and boys live in men's houses separate from all females. Each sex group (with the exception of small children) interacts only within itself, and antagonism between the two is shown on many ritual and other occasions. The sexual polarity pervades not only economic tasks and social roles, but the area of personality as well, where it takes the form of a concern with dominance and submission. Anxiety about people's ability to stay

149

within the prescribed sex roles and personality types, and about the real or imaginary desire to transcend them, is expressed in many pieces of folklore and ritual. It seems to be greater in the men than the women, a fact which the reporting ethnologist attributes to the ambivalent relationship men have with their mothers, and so with all women. (It may of course also be due to the awareness on the part of Mundurucu men that their dominance is based on precarious premises that could one day be reversed.) Whatever the reason, it is true that this sort of anxiety about even a temporary reversal of sex role is most likely to be found in societies where sex is an organising principle of social structure.

In Western societies today, sex *is* an organising principle of social structure, and, despite popular belief to the contrary, it plays a great part in determining social roles. So it is not surprising to find that, as among the Mundurucu, a great deal of anxiety in Western culture has its roots in the demands made by gender roles. Psychiatrists tell us that a great deal of our security as adults comes from staying within the boundaries of these roles—that we must stay within them if mental health is to be preserved. The psychiatrist Anthony Storr writes:

> ...in Western civilisation at the present time, men who consult a psychiatrist on account of emotional problems very commonly show too little aggression, whereas their feminine counterparts often exhibit too much...the pattern of the too-compliant male and the over-dominant female is so common that it accounts for a great deal of marital disharmony...Neurotic men complain of their wives' dominance, neurotic women of the husbands' lack of it...In such a marriage, each partner will generally show characteristics belonging to the opposite sex and will have failed to demarcate and define their respective roles in a partnership where the boundaries between male and female are blurred rather than accentuated...The emancipation of women is an inescapable fact...but we are far from having solved the problems created by women's

150

An old woman in New Guinea is ritually mocking the men's role. She has got hold of her husband's spear and stuck rubbish on the end of it, while the bag slung over her left shoulder mimics the masculine way of carrying loads. (Anthony Forge)

freedom....A confident belief in one's own masculinity or femininity is a fundamental part of human identity. **❞**

This fear certainly echoes the fears of ordinary people. For example, studies of attitudes towards the employment of women show that, bound up with people's beliefs about appropriate behaviour, is a fear that women will become 'masculinised' by employment, that they will become aggressive and dominant, and that family discord or breakdown will result. The UNESCO study quoted earlier found that 'The women themselves distrust their own aggressiveness which reveals itself when they acquire their new status—the harmony between man and wife is at stake, the possibility of true love seems to be less certain.'

As in the past, these fears arise at a time when changes in the roles of the sexes are seen to be imminent. In modern industrial society changes tend to be especially visible, since there is an emphasis on change rather than on the endurance of tradition; but in fact, despite 'emancipation' and despite the appearance of change in sex roles, fundamental differences between male and female work roles persist. Even where there is change, people often hold to traditional ways of thinking and behaving.

In all industrialised countries there is a marked differentiation by gender of most if not all occupations. One basic occupation in particular, that of housewife, is exclusively feminine. (The definition of 'housewife' here is 'the person in a household who is mainly responsible for the domestic duties'.) In Great Britain, 76% of all employed women are housewives, and so are 93% of non-employed women. The high percentage of housewives among the non-employed women is accounted for by the fact that many of them have children—nearly 60%, with 28% having children under two. Child care is, of course, an almost exclusively feminine task, both in the home and out of it. Mothers are responsible for the daily care of children, not fathers; females staff playgroups,

152

nurseries, primary schools and (to a lesser extent) secondary schools; nurses, including child nurses, are almost all females (the figure is 90% in Germany, Austria, Great Britain, Denmark, Norway, Switzerland, Finland and Greece). In fact most professional women are either nurses or teachers. In the United States females make up 86%, and in Great Britain 80%, of all primary school teachers.

Within industry there is a great deal of differentiation by sex. Most women, in all industrialised countries, are concentrated in textile and clothing manufacture and in food processing—usually between a third and two thirds of all working women are found in these industries. Since the Second World War, however, there has been spectacular growth in the employment of women in offices, so that in America, for instance, about 60% of working women are in white collar jobs. These secretarial jobs require a relatively short and inexpensive training and the behaviour they demand fits with the traditional female role: a male secretary except in certain high-level occupations such as the Civil Service, would be unthinkable in most countries. (Similarly, of course, the employment of women in factories producing domestic goods—textiles, clothes and food—reflects their conventional role.)

On the whole, males command the majority of jobs carrying high prestige, high skill and high income, and this is true throughout the industrial world. For example, of all professional scientific and technical qualifications gained by full-time students in Great Britain in 1969, men took 92% and women 8%. In the engineering and electrical industries in Britain in 1968, 17% of the men employed worked in semi-skilled jobs, but 48% of the women. Of all managers of large establishments tabulated for Britain in 1966, 87% were men and 13% women: of all foremen and supervisors 82% were men and 18% women. Women make up 3% of all barristers in the USA, 4% in Great Britain, and 7% in Sweden. A mere 0.06% of all engineers are female in Britain, 0.07% in the USA and 3.7% in France. While women in the professions receive the same rates of pay as men, in other jobs they do not: thus skill, prestige, financial reward and gender are interrelated in a complex but consistent fashion.

An index of this consistency—which has much to do with Western definitions of masculinity and femininity—is that in the United States in 1950 seven tenths of all working women were in twenty occupations, clustered around domestic and clerical work, nursing, teaching, and unskilled factory work. In Sweden, a country with a very contrasting history, the proportion in 1962 was exactly the same. In these twenty occupations in the United States only 12% of men were to be found; in Sweden, twelve years later, 11.9%. In both countries, and also in Britain, Belgium, Denmark, France, Germany, Italy, the Netherlands and Norway, two fifths of all working women were in five occupations. Much of the differentiation indicated by these figures has remained stable or even increased in recent years, despite the widespread belief that the sexes are becoming interchangeable through equal access to many occupations.

Apart from the jobs that men and women take up, there are other ways in which the statistics of employment show the impact of sex on social role.

Women's careers are characteristically discontinuous, whereas men's are not. A significant proportion of the female industrial labour force consists of part-time workers—at least 10% in Canada and Federal Germany, 18% in Britain, and more than 20% in Sweden, Denmark and the United States. The tendency to choose part-time work is a reflection of women's domestic responsibilities; in one sample, 18% of women working full time had children under sixteen, against 53% of those working part time. Domestic responsibility usually means that a woman has to give up work completely for several years at a time, and only return to it gradually. Pauline Pinder, in a survey undertaken for Political and Economic Planning in 1969, described the difference between the careers of men and women:

❛ The average man's working life extends uninterruptedly from the end of school or training until retirement; but the average woman is increasingly likely to have a three phase working life: the first, from leaving school to the birth of her first child, when she will normally work full time; the second, while her children are young, when she may withdraw wholly or partly from the labour force; the third, from the time the youngest child goes to school until she reaches the age of retirement, during which she will probably return to fulltime work. ❜

It is not just in the rhythms of their careers that men and women differ. There are extensive differences bound up with the general roles of the sexes and with the expectations and opportunities they lead to. Tradition and prejudice continue to affect these opportunities, so that jobs which are traditionally feminine tend to remain so—usually through some rationalisation about their suitability for women. The young woman deciding on a job or career will tend to reject (or be rejected by) 'masculine' occupations and consider only those to which she has easy access as potential sources of satisfaction. Here she will be greatly influenced by her upbringing, which will equip her better for jobs that demand the sort of 'feminine' character traits that, as we saw in Chapter 2, are likely to be instilled in her. The effect of this is made still stonger by the fact that breaking into a man's occupation in itself demands a good share of the 'masculine' virtues of initiative, effort and aggressiveness.

Finally there is her education—a more potent factor in forming sex differences than most people are ready to admit. In theory, education is supposed to be equally available to males and females in our contemporary industrial society, and this is thought to be one of the most concrete effects of postwar democratic ideology and of twentieth-century female emancipation. What are the facts?

At the primary and secondary levels the number of girls at school is nearly (though not quite) in proportion to their numbers in the population as a whole. In North America in 1963, for example, girls made up 48.4% of primary school pupils and 49.4% of secondary school pupils although females outnumber males as a whole.

At the lowest end of education there is a persistent tendency for illiteracy to be more frequent in females than in males. In Greece, 30% of women are illiterate compared with 8% of men; in Yugoslavia, 34% of women and 12% of men; in Spain, 18% of women and 8% of men.

But it is at the highest levels of education that the disparity is most marked. For every hundred people aged twenty to twenty-four in higher education in 1965 there were 6.6 females in the United Kingdom, 5.3 in Denmark, 2.3 in Switzerland and 15.2 in Bulgaria. While women made up about two fifths of the intake of university students in Britain in 1967, women take less than a third of all final degrees and only about one ninth of all higher degrees.

These facts clearly reflect the belief that education is more important for a boy than it is for a girl—as indeed it is in a society where 'work' is the activity of all adult men but only some women. And it is not merely in the numbers receiving an education that gender plays a part: it also influences the subjects they study. In the United States in 1964, 46% of Masters' degrees in education were gained by women but only 10% of these in science. Of all those studying medicine, dentistry and health in Britain in 1967, two thirds were men. Similar disproportions can be found elsewhere.

To sum up, then, we can say that the chief importance of biological sex in determining social roles is in providing a universal and obvious division around which other distinctions can be organised. In deciding which activities are to fall on each side of the boundary, the important factor is culture. In early upbringing, in education and in their adult occupations, males and females are pressed by our society into different moulds. At the end of this process it is not surprising that they come to regard their distinctive occupations as predetermined by some general law, despite the fact that in reality the biological differences between the sexes are neither so large nor so invariable as most of us suppose, and despite the way in which other cultures have developed sex roles quite different from our own, which seem just as natural and just as inevitable to them as ours do to us.

6

Sex and gender

'Sex' is a biological term: 'gender' a psychological and cultural one. Common sense suggests that they are merely two ways of looking at the same division and that someone who belongs to, say, the female sex will automatically belong to the corresponding (feminine) gender. In reality this is not so. To be a man or a woman, a boy or a girl, is as much a function of dress, gesture, occupation, social network and personality, as it is of possessing a particular set of genitals.

This rather surprising contention is supported by a number of facts. First, anthropologists have reported wide variation in the way different cultures define gender. It is true that every society uses biological sex as a criterion for the ascription of gender but, beyond that simple starting point, no two cultures would agree completely on what distinguishes one gender from the other. Needless to say, every society believes that its own definitions of gender correspond to the biological duality of sex.

Culturally, therefore, one finds the same biological distinctions between male and female coexisting with great variations in gender roles. By contrast one also finds individual people whose culturally defined genders coexist with indeterminate sex. These people are the intersexed, and recent studies of them in Britain and the United States have shown that someone who is neither male or female can be masculine or feminine—just as masculine or just as feminine as those who are biologically normal. If proof is needed that sex and gender are two separate entities then this is it, and indeed some other societies tacitly admit the failure of any simple dual classification by recognising not two but three sexual categories.

Dr Robert Stoller, in his book 'Sex and Gender', defines the relationship between the two as follows:

❛ ...with a few exceptions, there are two sexes, male and female. To determine sex one must assay the following physical conditions: chromosomes, external genitalia, internal genitalia, gonads, hormonal states, and secondary sex characteristics...One's sex, then, is determined by an algebraic sum of all these qualities, and, as is obvious, most people fall under one of two separate bell curves, the one of which is called 'male', the other 'female'...

Gender is a term that has psychological and cultural rather than biological connotations; if the proper terms for sex are 'male' and 'female', the corresponding terms for gender are 'masculine' and 'feminine'; these latter may be quite independent of (biological) sex. Gender is the amount of masculinity or femininity found in a person, and, obviously, while there are mixtures of both in many humans, the normal male has a preponderance of masculinity and the normal female a preponderance of femininity. *

Stoller is a psychoanalyst who specialises in problems of gender identity, and his book results from the detailed study of 85 patients. Other workers in this field are Dr John Money and Drs John and Joan Hampson, who have all worked in the Endocrine clinic of the Johns Hopkins Hospital in the United States on what have been called 'experiments in nature'—that is, patients who have a disorder of biological sex and are to some degree hermaphroditic. While Stoller talks about 'gender identity', Money and the Hampsons refer to 'psychosexual orientation': the meaning of both terms is the sense an individual has of himself or herself as male or female, of belonging to one or other group. The development of this sense is essentially the same for both biologically normal and abnormal individuals, but the study of the biologically abnormal can tell us a great deal about the relative parts played by biology and social rearing: there are a multitude of ways in which it can illuminate the debate about the origin of sex differences.

To start with what is perhaps the most striking finding, boys without penises may become 'normal' males: girls with penises and without uteruses may become 'normal' females. Stoller compares the gender development of two American boys, both born without penises but, in the strictly genetic sense, normal. In one case, the child was four when Stoller saw him and was considered by experts and laymen alike, including his family, to be a 'psychologically' normal (i.e. masculine) boy. He was rough and active, enjoying football and baseball with his father and wrestling with his siblings. He wanted to be a wrestler when he grew up. He disliked anything that looked girlish: he played at being Superman. He combed his hair like his father and collected toy guns as his father collected real ones. His father was the manager of a garage and the child's own favourite game was 'Gas Station'—digging in the dirt, building a garage with bricks and using the cat's tail as a petrol pump. He did not doubt that he was male, and his behaviour, interests, appearance and mannerisms all confirmed this basic gender identity.

The second case, seen by Stoller at the age of fifteen, also lacked a penis. He was a very disturbed child, essentially male in his gender identity but painfully aware of his defect. The question for him was 'If I am defective, can I be a proper male?' Since the age of seven, he had played a homosexual game with other boys that centred on his defect. Both children in this game pulled each other's penises in order to produce pain, at which point they cried out. Since the patient felt no pain in the lump of skin that was his 'penis' his cry was only a pretence; but, although both children knew this, the game served its purpose of bolstering the patient's sense of maleness by proving his penis temporarily as 'real' as those of normal boys.

The crucial difference between these two cases was not one of biology: both were defective as biological males. The lack of defect in the gender identity of the first child was due to his parents' attitudes in rearing him: they treated him as a normal boy, expected him to behave as one and provided him with 'good' masculine and feminine models themselves. The parents of the second boy were not particularly good models of masculinity and femininity, nor did they expect normal masculine behaviour in their child as a matter of course. They transmitted to him their belief that he was a biological anomaly who could not rightfully belong to either sex or either gender.

These cases show the critical role played by parental expectations in the development of a child's gender identity. They show also that a child can achieve a firm gender identity as a male even if he lacks the prime insignia of maleness, a penis. The child senses that gender is not necessarily defined by sex, and indeed studies of children in general have shown that they do not use anatomy as a criterion of sex, at least at first. Until about six or seven, children will declare that girls can become boys or vice versa provided they adopt the right games, clothes, haircuts and so on. This has usually been taken to show a lack of biological knowledge in the child, but in fact it is probably a realistic assessment of the situation, incorporating the perception that gender is socially and not biologically defined. When we react to someone as male or female we do not need to see if he or she has a penis or vagina, breasts or a hairy chest. Mostly the social situation defines gender (wife=woman, dentist=man, and so on) or gender is visible as a sum of qualities, including mannerism, way of speaking, dress, choice of topics in conversation and so on. Gender is a visible fact most of the time: sex is not.

Of course the four-year-old without a penis is likely to encounter problems when he reaches adolescence, as the fifteen-year-old was already doing. When he is of the age to have sexual relationships he is bound to run up against the fact that the penis is supposed to be the essential accessory of successful maleness. This is, after all, the near-universal belief. But is it true? The literature recounts the case of one female, reared as a male, and male in 'her' gender identity, who was spectacularly successful even as a lover. She made an artificial penis for herself and with its help was capable of intercourse—so convincingly capable, indeed, that the girl to whom she made love accused her of getting her pregnant. This sort of observation led Stoller to conclude that sexual satisfaction does not depend on a fixed biological sexuality working through behaviour of the appropriate gender. Rather it is the other way around: 'With other patients we have seen with anatomical defects in their genitalia, as well as with anatomically normal people, it is clear that sexual satisfaction serves to establish and maintain one's gender identity.'

The experience of sexual satisfaction itself can be a function of gender role rather than biological sex, when the two are discordant. One of Stoller's patients, a biologically normal female who had a male gender identity, wrote:

'During my sexual relationship with a woman, I actually feel as though I have a penis. I feel totally masculine and superior to the female I'm with. When I experience an orgasm I feel that I ejaculate. It's difficult to explain. My orgasm is not a single feeling but more of a spasmodic sensation. I can have sexual relations with a woman, have one orgasm and be completely satisfied. When I have intercourse with a man, I have to have several orgasms before I can relax and feel satisfied. '

This woman has two kinds of orgasmic response: one male, the other female. The ability to have several orgasms in succession is a female characteristic (see the findings of Masters and Johnson cited in Chapter 4) and it is significant that this woman's gender identity seems to override her biological capacity to be multiorgasmic when she is having sexual relations with another woman.

It follows logically from this that the vagina and the penis are valued (by normal people) and demanded (by abnormal people who lack them) as concrete symbols of femininity and masculinity, rather than masculinity and femininity arising automatically from the mere possession of these organs. A short case history of one intersexed 'female' illustrates this point.

One of Stoller's patients, who was as biologically neuter as a human can be, first went to see him at the age of eighteen because 'her' breasts had failed to develop and menstruation had not started. She had the chromosomonal make-up XO, and while her external genitalia appeared to be feminine she had no uterus, vagina, or gonads. However she had been reared as a female and no one in the family had any doubts that she was a female. Stoller reports that at the time of her first consultation she was unremarkably feminine in her behaviour and dress, and in her social and sexual desires and fantasies: in these ways she was just like other girls in Southern California. On diagnosis she was told she would never be able to have children and that she lacked a vagina, but that she could be given one by plastic surgery. During the course of psychiatric treatment (for the possible trauma of this discovery) three aspects of her feminine identification were revealed: firstly, her desire to marry and have children; secondly, her concern over the appearance and function of her genitalia; thirdly, her feminine interests in appearance, games, use of leisure, sexual relationships and so on. Her elder sister said of her:

   'She had a doll that she got when she was 8, and she always said that she was going to save it to give to her little girl after she got married. She still has that doll and it's in perfect condition...She was 9 years old when my son was born and she always loved to take care of him, and was very, very good at handling him...You can't kid her about not having children.'

The patient was concerned about her lack of a vagina, and wished to have one constructed. But her parents opposed this: she was not married at the time, and they felt it would lead to 'promiscuity'—although they knew she could not become pregnant since she had neither womb nor ovaries. Their treatment of their 'daughter' as a normal female illustrates well the view of sexuality as merely one aspect of gender-appropriate behaviour. This individual was biologically no more female than male but, since she had been reared as a female, she wanted a vagina as a confirmation of her femininity; furthermore, everyone 'knew' she was female, so feminine norms applied to her behaviour—hence the 'double standard' morality advanced as a reason for delaying surgery. In fact, the parents were eventually overruled by medical experts and the patient got her vagina, slept with her boyfriend, married, and led a 'normal' life as a woman.

Case studies of individuals, though fascinating, cannot alone support sweeping generalisations about the lack of identity between sex and gender. A large group of hermaphroditic patients have been studied by Money and the Hampsons, and in 95% of all the cases (totalling 113, which is a large number for this sort of abnormality) *the sex of rearing corresponded to gender identity.* Most significantly, the correspondence held even for those individuals whose sex of rearing contradicted their biological sex as determined by chromosomes, hormones, gonads and the formations of the internal and external genitals.

The classic instances of this amazing finding are provided by two of the patients in the group. Both are cases of the adrenogenital syndrome—children born with internal female organs, but masculinised external genitalia. Both are female in the sense of chromosomal sex: both have the outward appearance of maleness. One was reared as a girl and one as a boy: one consequently has a female gender identity— believes 'herself' to be female—while the other has a male gender identity and is convinced 'he' is a male.

Thus the most important conclusion to be drawn from the study of hermaphroditic individuals is that gender identity is established early and usually irreversibly. Clinical experience shows that a change of sex of rearing of a child can be successful if undertaken before the age of two years, but that after this the risks increase. Change after four usually causes severe maladjustment. The conclusion is that, in both biologically normal and abnormal individuals, gender identity is fundamentally established in more or less the same period as native language—in the first two years of life.

164

This evidence therefore disproves Freud's insistence on the early bisexuality of both male and female. Also, if it does not actually disprove, it certainly fails to confirm many theories about the innateness of masculine and feminine behaviour traits, personality qualities and sexual proclivities. The masculine child without a penis, the feminine male who walks, crosses 'her' legs and blows 'her' nose like a woman, the single-chromosome neuter who has fantasies of childbearing with pathetic and unrelenting persistence, the chromosomal male whose gonads secrete oestrogens and produce breasts, thus confusing the social diagnosis of masculinity—all these show gender identity to be an independent cultural variable. The most pressing question physicians ask of these people when they present themselves for treatment is not 'Are you a male or a female?' but 'Do you feel yourself to be male or female?' Gender identity (feeling oneself to be male or female) is the crucial determinant of gender role (living as a male or female); biological sex can be and often is reconstructed to allow the individual to play his or her gender role without confusion and risk of social ridicule. Here it is biology that is plastic in the literal sense, and altered to conform with identity: not identity that is shaped by biology.

There are many points at which the study of intersexuals throws light on the nature-nurture controversy, and they are too valuable to be ignored. For example, intersexed patients reared as females have strong feminine fantasy lives and characteristically feminine erotic inclinations despite the virtually total absence of female hormones. These are the patients with an XO chromosomal make-up. They have no functioning gonadal tissue at all, and therefore no ovarian oestrogenic hormones. Thirteen of these female-reared patients in the Hampsons and Money series all had daydreams and fantasies of romantic courtship, marriage and heterosexual erotic play, just like their normal female peers.

This relationship between sex hormones and eroticism has been a constant theme in the literature on sex differences. Therese Benedek for instance claimed to have shown in 1952 that the hormonal changes in the menstrual cycle are related to the content of dreams. But Dr Hampson, surveying the group of 31 patients in the Johns Hopkins sample whose sex of rearing contradicted their hormonal sex, comes to the considered opinion that these patients provide no convincing evidence that sex hormones act as a single causal agent in the establishment of gender role and psychosexual orientation. Doctors treating hermaphroditic patients have found cognitional eroticism (erotic imagery, fantasies and dreams) to be yet another variable of gender and, as such, independent of hormonal level or function. Dr John Money, writing on 'Sex hormones and other variables in human eroticism', says:

‘ Just as nonhealthy eroticism may become indelibly imprinted, so also may healthy eroticism, masculine and feminine. Indeed, so fixed is masculinity and femininity of outlook in healthy men and women respectively, that it has always been assumed that sexual orientation must be determined in some automatic fashion utterly independent of life experience, for example, by genes or hormones. Now it becomes necessary to allow that erotic outlook and orientation is an autonomous psychologic phenomenon, independent of genes and hormones, and moreover, a permanent and ineradicable one as well. ’

Another area in which the case history of an intersexual touches the general debate about the origin of sex differences is that of intellectual achievement. A male patient reared as a female reinforces a theory proposed to explain female underachievement; this patient first came for consultation when male secondary sex characteristics began to develop in adolescence (and he still thought he was female). Laboratory tests revealed maleness and the child was told of this: then followed his social conversion from female to male. Part of this conversion was a dramatic change of his school record. Instead of being a 'mediocre' student he became an 'excellent' one. Significantly, he began to be top of his class at mathematics, a subject in which he had done very poorly when he thought he was a girl. In other words, his school achievement had been partly determined by his awareness of the sexually appropriate norms of achievement and it is this sort of awareness that underlies female underachievement in the academic field generally.

Just as we can learn important lessons from the study of intersexuals about how prople acquire their gender identities, so too we can from the study of transsexuals and homosexuals.

There has been considerable confusion over such terms as 'intersexual', 'transsexual' and 'homosexual' due mostly to lack of knowledge, but as more precise studies emerge it has become possible to define and use these terms with greater accuracy. 'Intersexual' refers to a biological condition; the terms 'transsexual' and 'homosexual' both refer to gender disorders—that is, disorders in the social-cultural acquisition of gender role and gender identity. In the aetiology of both transsexualism and homosexuality strong cross-sex identification is an important factor: both male transsexuals and male homosexuals have identified with their mothers to an extent not found in 'normal' people; neither has substituted father-identification for mother-identification, a process which is basic to normal masculinity. In the case of homosexuality, one significant component of gender role, eroticism, is out of step with all the other variables of sex and gender. The homosexual man feels he is a male but cannot behave like one erotically. While unusually artistic and creative men may have identified with their mothers to a greater extent than usual, they have selected for identification specifically the non-erotic elements. Homosexuals have carried the identification further, and been unable to separate themselves as men from the eroticism of their mothers, which is directed towards males.

For transsexuals, however, gender identity and

gender role completely contradict the variables of biological sex and the variable of sex of rearing. The transsexual male feels he is a female, and so denies he is a homosexual: to him, his sexual relations with other males are not aberrant but normal. Transsexuals have not made the break with the mother at any point: they have no sense of their gender identity (or even of their self identity) as separate from that of their mothers, and they duplicate their mothers' femininity in areas extending from the narrowly sexual to the visibly cultural—in dress, activity and mannerism.

The case histories of child transsexuals show the cross-sex gender identity to be noticeable very early in childhood, sometimes by one year. (This agrees with the findings of Money and the Hampsons that gender identity is well established by the age of two.) Three such boys, brought for psychiatric evaluation at the ages of four and five, all dressed and behaved like little girls, had girls' interests and enjoyed girls' activities, and their mothers encouraged this femininity. The fathers of all three were physically absent from their families most of the time. The involvement of child transsexuals with their mothers seems to be physical as well as emotional and psychosexual, and these mothers kept their children physically close to them: the blurring of ego boundaries between mother and child was also the blurring of physical boundaries. This is a similar phenomenon to that noted by David Levy in his study of 'Maternal Overprotection', in which the symbiosis between mother and child is continued late into childhood. Normally, of course, it is given up as the child acquires his or her own gender and self identity in the first three or four years of life. Both David Levy and Stoller independently observe the heightened artistic 'feminine' abilities of these boys. Sounds and smells, colours, patterns, music, were all responded to intensely. Stoller comments:

❝ It is not surprising that the artistic interests of these little boys are those our society considers more feminine than masculine, for while the boys are intelligent, active, curious, and original, their creativity is sensual not intellectual. They touch, stroke, smell, hear, look and taste—they create to please their sense. They are not interested in mathematics, the function of machines, construction or logic—precisions of the mind. These observations are in keeping with similar findings in adult men, in whom one also much more frequently finds severe disturbances in gender identity among creative artists than with creative theoretical and applied scientists. **,**

Like other processes which occur spontaneously and unproblematically in the vast majority of cases (pregnancy for instance) the development of gender identity is not usually studied in its normal, non-pathological state. Cases of unusual development come forward as medical or psychiatric specialties; cases of normal development do not come forward at all. However, research in many areas has shown that processes integral to normal development of gender identity also occur in abnormal development, but with certain significant distortions.

The core of the process is identification. Males usually identify with males and females with females, and so normal male and female gender identities are formed. However, where a male identifies with a female in a persistent and inflexible way, disorders such as homosexuality and transsexuality are more likely to arise.

The discussion above, like most discussions of disorders of gender identity, is concerned with males. While the reported incidence of these disorders in the female is lower than in the male, this fact should not be allowed to conceal the finding that, where female homosexuality and transsexuality arise, their aetiologies seem to run exactly parallel with those of the same disorders in the male. In other words, both homosexuality and transsexuality in females are due to strong masculine identification. This in turn suggests a reason for their lower incidence in the female: the male is more likely to be thwarted in his attempt to become thoroughly masculine, since in our society it is the father rather than the mother who is likely to be absent or remote. It is, of course, perfectly possible that girls reared without fathers are more feminine than those reared with fathers, but femininity in a girl is nothing remarkable.

One problem remains: does biology play any role at all in determining the development of gender identity in normal individuals? The consensus of opinion seems to be that its role is a minimal one, in that the biological predisposition to a male or female gender identity (if such a condition exists) may be decisively and ineradicably overridden by cultural learning. Those who have worked in the field of hermaphroditic disorders and problems of gender identity seem very impressed by the power of culture to ignore biology altogether.

On the other hand, there is the evidence of other medical research to suggest that biological sex-differentiation extends beyond gonad and hormone to the interior structures of the brain and thus to the controlling centres of behaviour.

Experiments with mammals have shown that hormone implants in the brain have the capacity to affect sexual behaviour significantly. What appears to happen is that hormone concentrations in particular brain areas stimulate patterns of behaviour: for instance, in the squirrel monkey penile erections can be produced in this way. Hormone implants offer the opportunity to connect specific brain locations with items of behaviour. Although this cannot be done in man, the reported association between dreaming rapid-eye-movement sleep and spontaneous penile erection suggests the same link between sexual arousal and localised brain activity.

The hypothesis that in mammals the central nervous system itself is differentiated into male and female by the action of hormones in the critical period before or just after birth was mentioned in Chapter 1. This hypothesis is not contradicted by some of the evidence presented since the mid 1950s by the Hampsons and Money in their study of hermaphroditic and pseudohermaphroditic individuals. On that basis, biological abnormalities would have caused the hormones to function abnormally and to fail to differentiate the central nervous systems of these patients by sex. This would then provide an endocrinological basis for bisexuality, that is, for the development of either male or female gender identity. Some evidence exists that intersexed people more often have disturbances in gender identity than the rest of the normally sexed population. However, the suggestion that there is a neural-hormonal basis existing for these disturbances can be countered by the reminder that such people often have tremendous psychological problems to contend with, including an ambiguous body image and the ridicule of their peers. Moreover it is clear from the study of child transsexuals that a cross-sex gender identity can be acquired quite untraumatically by people with no biological sex abnormality of any kind.

Research with other mammals, though fascinating, can only be applied hypothetically to the study of humans. Particularly in this field of sexual behaviour, animals are subject to a much more direct control by the instinctive part of the brain than human beings. For instance, if the vagina of a cat is artifically stimulated she will display the characteristic 'after reaction' which follows mating behaviour—throwing off the male, rolling over, and licking the vaginal area. The stimulation of the erogenous zone triggers off a particular pattern of behaviour. There is no comparable chain of event and reaction in humans.

It seems clear that, as man has evolved from the primates, his behaviour has come to be less and less under the control of biological (hormonal, neural) factors. The cerebrum and cerebral activity are human specialisations. Thus the human female is not sexually receptive only at a particular hormonal phase of the reproductive cycle: she is receptive all the time—or rather when she chooses to be—although the possibility of conception remains closely controlled by hormonal cycles. Perhaps this is an instructive example of how, even in humans, hormones have a necessary (though not sufficient) role to play in the evolution of gender identity within the limits set by biological sex.

7
The learning of gender roles

A newborn baby is not only classified immediately by sex: it is also assigned a gender. In most maternity hospitals sex-typed comments on the behaviour and appearance of newborns are aired within a few moments of birth. The male baby who has an erection while being weighed is referred to jokingly as 'a dirty little man': the female baby born with curly hair is told she is pretty, and some hospitals keep pink and blue blankets for girls and boys. All these responses mark the beginning of a gender-learning process which is critically important for the child.

This chapter looks at the exact ways in which gender is learnt—at the social mechanisms and personal responses involved. It examines how masculinity and femininity of personality, behaviour, attitudes and roles evolve with the culturally-provided experience of gender learning.

Even with newborn babies, mothers differentiate between boys and girls in their behaviour towards them. A study by H A Moss showed that at three weeks of age mothers held male infants 27 minutes more per eight hours than females: at three months, 14 minutes longer. How far is it reasonable to interpret the mother's behaviour as a gender-role lesson for the child, based on her own life-long distinctions between masculinity and femininity? In one way the mother was responding directly to the infant's behaviour. The male babies in this sample slept less than the females and were more irritable—they cried and fussed for a greater proportion of the time—and the explanation of this may lie in the male's greater vulnerability to difficulties in birth, resulting in chronic irritability during the first weeks of life. (Evidence from a large-scale study confirms the fact that more males than females have behavioural disorders related to complications in pregnancy and delivery.) But is this the whole answer? Even with babies who were in the same state (awake or asleep, crying or not crying) the mothers tended to stimulate and arouse the males more, both by tactile and visual stimulation. Conversely they responded to the girls by imitation more than they did to the boys—repeating the babies' actions and noises back to them. This is direct evidence of a maternal tendency to reinforce behaviour differently in the two sexes and it may perhaps help to explain the verbal superiority of the female: if female babies receive imitative reinforcement of their early noises, this may continue into a more highly verbal relationship with the mother than the male child has.

The mother's response to the male child's irritability decreases as he gets older, and she makes less of an attempt to soothe him. The explanation of this offered by Moss is that the mother initiates a pattern, in keeping with cultural expectations, according to which males are more assertive and less responsive to socialisation than females. Intractable irritability is classified by the mother as an expression of 'maleness' which she neither can nor wants to do anything about. The data support this: whatever the origin of the male's greater irritability (whether innate or not) by the age of three months the mother has amplified this tendency in her own response to the baby, so reinforcing it. As for the finding that males receive greater stimulation, this too could produce sex differences: the quality of stimulation received in the early months can have a significant effect on many aspects of development.

Lois Murphy, in a study of child-rearing, also notes differences in the maternal treatment of boy and girl babies. Mothers appear to treat boys with respect for their autonomy, following the baby's own rhythm and adopting a 'come and get it' attitude. Girls are more hovered over and fiddled with, on the lines of 'mother knows best'.

The way in which very young children pick up their gender roles is not principally verbal or disciplinary (as it is later) but kinaesthetic. Moss's study, although small-scale, is virtually the only carefully controlled, systematic study of this kinaesthetic differentiation by mothers. It ties in with the first of the four processes that Ruth Hartley believes to be central to the development of gender roles. These processes are socialisation by manipulation, canalisation, verbal appellation, and activity exposure. All four processes are differentiated by sex, and all are features of the child's socialisation from birth on.

The first process (manipulation) was observed by Hartley in children aged from one to five in 22 families. An example of it is the mother's tendency to 'fuss with' the baby girl's hair, dress her in feminine fashion and tell her how pretty she is. Hartley suggests this is essentially the same process as the 'moulding' of infants observed by anthropologists in other cultures. 'Moulding' or 'manipulation' has an enduring effect because the child subsumes the mother's view of her (as 'pretty', as 'feminine') in her own concept of herself.

Canalisation, the second process, involves directing the attention of male and female children onto particular objects or aspects of objects. Sex-differentiated toys, for example, are an early feature of the child's world, and the opportunity to play with them (and to be rewarded for playing with them in the appropriate way) lays a basis for the adult's pleasure in the things these toys represent. Thus, part of the so-called maternal response may well be the anticipated pleasure females feel in duplicating as mothers the pleasures they received during childhood doll play. Piaget has shown how familiarisation with an object can itself act to provoke positive responses. If children have played with dolls, miniature washing machines and soft toys, or on the other hand with guns, cars and bricks, then objects of these types will have an emotional advantage. The sex-typed objects which play an important part in the child's 'rehearsal' of its gender role will keep their advantage in later life if the child's response to them is reinforced, which it almost invariably is.

Verbal appellations, the third of the four processes, have a capacity, often unnoticed, to be sex-typed too. ('You're a naughty boy.' 'That's a good girl.') Data collected by Hartley and others show that this sort of remark acts as a sign leading to a concept of self-identity in which sex is inbuilt. The child learns to think of himself or herself as male or female, and so to identify with all other males or females.

Mothers and fathers transmit aspects of gender role directly in the way they talk even to very young children. For instance, boys and girls are told which postures they should adopt during urination: the notion that the male should stand up while the female should sit down is not one that naturally occurs to the child on its own. Two-year-old girls who persistently urinate on the floor because they adopt their brothers' position whilst lacking his anatomical equipment, are much more likely simply to have temporarily failed to pick up this aspect of their gender role than to be manifesting the early signs of penis envy.

The last process is that of activity exposure. Both male and female children are exposed to traditional masculine and feminine activities, and the exposure of both sexes to female domestic activity might seem as likely to produce domesticity among males as it is among females. However, there is evidence that mothers encourage the female child's identification with this aspect of gender role as part of a permanent process in which the child's imitations are a stop gap until she becomes adult and can act out her domesticity in reality: for boys, the identification is short-lived, discouraged, and in no way held out to them as an enduring aspect of their gender role. Sears, Maccoby and Levin show that American mothers distinguish between the kind of chores assigned to boys and girls even with five-year-olds. Cleaning the dishes, making the beds, and laying the table are girls' work; emptying rubbish, cleaning ash trays and emptying waste baskets are for boys. (So the male's domestic responsibilities even at the age of five are those which take him outside the home, rather than confining him within it, even if these first trips are only to the dustbin.)

How does the child respond to all this? What evidence is there that it does in fact make use of such adult behaviour in learning its gender role?

First of all, it is important to remember that the

parents may take part in all these processes with very little, if any, awareness of what they are doing. Sears, Maccoby and Levin, in their 'Patterns of Child Rearing', report that

6 ...many mothers did not recognise any efforts they might be making to produce appropriate sex role behaviour. When they did see differences in their own behaviour—and some who had both sons and daughters did—they tended to interpret such differences as natural reactions to innate differences between boys and girls. They thought a mother had to adjust her behaviour to the sex-determined temperament of her child, but did not consider that her own actions might be responsible for any such characteristics. 9

This unawareness on the part of mothers of the moulding effect of their behaviour coexisted with a strong tendency, noted by Sears, Maccoby and Levin, to differentiate activities and techniques for training and disciplining boys and girls.

Ruth Hartley says that 'From the young subject's point of view, sex role, child role, and self definition are blended in an unselfconscious complex of unobstructed behaviours.' The important word here—'unselfconscious'—stresses again the absence of awareness, this time on the part of the child. Whatever it is that the child learns, he or she is not aware of learning it, nor aware of its content and implications.

As for the effects of these processes, a multitude of studies agree that by the age of four children have a firm knowledge of sex identity and are well able to perceive distinctions of gender role. Meyer Rabban found in his study of 'Sex Role Identification in Young Children' that by this age children identified their own sex correctly and many were capable of achieving 100% correctness in choosing sex-appropriate toys. (A list of such sex-appropriate toys was given in Table 3, Chapter 2.)

In guiding their children's choice of toys, parents

may be either explicit in their intention to foster the development of appropriate gender roles, or unaware that they are doing anything at all to encourage it. Meyer Rabban took a number of case studies from his main sample of children, and asked mothers what, if anything, they did to encourage sex-typing and gender-role development in their children through toy play. The mother of one boy who made 100% sex-correct toy choices said 'I would actively encourage boyish play, put away dolls.' The mother of another boy who always chose the appropriate toy said to her son in the interview 'Dolls are for girls, not for boys. Everybody will think you are a sissy. You should play with cars and trucks.' To the interviewer: 'We bought him a truck for Christmas.' But the mother of a boy who chose inappropriate toys said she didn't think a boys's participation in girls' games mattered. A girl in a similar situation played with her father regularly and chose all boys' toys; her mother reported that she wasn't bothered by this attachment to male toys.

A child's ability to select sex-appropriate toys, or rather his established preference for them, is a signal that he has acquired the solid foundations of an appropriate and irreversible gender role. This is not a straightforward procedure, nor is it the same for both sexes. Studies of children indicate that the boy's development of gender identity is more problematic and causes him more anxiety than that of the girl. Again, this underlines the cultural nature of gender-role definition, and reflects the common-sense observation that boys find it harder to grow into men because they are brought up by women.

One difference between the sexes from the ages of four to nine is that girls adhere less consistently and specifically to the roles, activities and objects of their sex. At four and five, boys are more clearly aware of the sex-appropriateness of toys in adult eyes. There is a class difference too: middle-class boys and working-class children of both sexes have learnt this aspect of their gender roles sooner than middle-class girls (who, according to research, are under less pressure to conform to their gender role). From six to nine, girls are particularly liable to show preferences for the masculine role. This does not mean that they are not identifying themselves with the feminine role, but rather that girls have fewer social inhibitions about showing cross-sex interests and preferences. A boy's deviation is 'sissy' whereas a girl is merely 'a tomboy'—a phase she will easily grow out of when she needs to. In contrast to girls, boys both are in fact, and are encouraged to be, consistently masculine in their gender roles from early childhood on. It seems to be fathers and not mothers who focus anxiety on this matter.

Gender roles and gender identities are not acquired mechanically by the child from the parent, but because the child identifies with the parent in a variety of ways. Principally it seems that the child wants to be like the parent, and hence is motivated to act like him or her; the child classes himself in the same gender group as the parent, and for this reason imitates the relevant items of behaviour, at first unconsciously and later consciously. Both 'imitation' and 'identification' refer to the tendency for a person to reproduce the actions, attitudes and emotional responses exhibited by real life or symbolic models.

There are 'chicken and egg' debates about which comes first—the child's knowledge of his sex or his perception that his parents expect and reward the sort of behaviour appropriate to that sex. The social-learning view is that for the child the chain of reasoning is: 'I want rewards, I am rewarded for doing boy (girl) things, therefore I want to be a boy (girl).' The cognitive view is the other way around: 'I am a boy (girl), therefore I want to do boy (girl) things, therefore the opportunity to do boy (girl) things, and be approved of, is rewarding.'

The cognitive view would accord with the results of some research which shows that the maturation of the feeling 'I am a boy' or 'I am a girl', and the ability to identify with males and females as social groups, may be partly a function of the child's cognitive development—of his ability to conceptualise. Research has recently indicated that children definitely conceive of their gender identities as fixed and unchangeable in the same way and at the same time as they are able to understand the invariable identity of physical objects. However, while these cognitive powers arise in the child through a process of maturation, the definitions of gender that the child arrives at by using them are socially determined (as we saw from the the studies of intersexuals and transsexuals). Also, it cannot be shown that the feeling 'I am a boy' precedes the desire to play the boy-role and obtain its rewards. The gender identities of children vary with the kind of families they live in, the personalities of their parents and the way their parents behave towards them.

Freudian theory differs from both the cognitive and the social-learning theories by making the development of gender identity dependent on the evolution of a specifically sexual consciousness of self as male or female. According to Freud 'sexuality' is the core meaning of both sex and gender. 'Identification' means for Freud an emotional tie, and it emerges as a means of resolving the Oedipus complex—the boy identifies with the father because he fears his father as an aggressor (the obstacle in the path of his sexual attachment to the mother and the protagonist in the drama of castration anxiety). Since the little girl neither fears castration nor is sexually attached to the mother, the basis of her identification with the mother is different from the boy's with the father. It is based on her fear that she might lose her mother's love. The objection to this Freudian view lies in the incontrovertible evidence that gender role is irreversibly acquired before the age of three, that is before the Oedipal conflict is supposed to set in. The sex differences in the child's identification with the parent are not due to Oedipal difficulties but to the structure of the family; what Freud perceived was that the female child's acquisition of gender identity is a far less problematic process, due to the more or less continuous relationship with the mother, while the male child, in sensing his 'otherness' from the mother, must then take the relatively absent and emotionally distant father as a model for his behaviour.

From studies correlating children's gender identities with a multitude of factors, it is clear that their development is very strongly influenced by the relative power of the two parents, the way each takes part in caring for the child and their techniques of discipline.

In building up its gender role, a child tends to imitate and to identify with the more powerful parent, whether mother or father. Various researchers have shown that where parents differ in their power, authority, or control over resources, both boys and girls imitate the behaviour of the parent with most power. In fact, the similarity between mother and son in mother-dominant homes is as close as the similarity between father and son in father-dominant homes. Punishment and discipline are only important as an index of power, not in themselves. A mother or father who is both powerful and punitive in a manner disagreeable to the child, is more likely to be imitated than a parent who punishes in the same way but is seen by the child as lacking power. The child's perception of who has the most power seems most often to be based on economic factors, so that the father who earns money appears more powerful than the mother who spends it. In one experiment, the tendency was for the children to imitate the model who controlled the resources in question, not the one who received them. The same phenomenon, of identification on the basis of power, is found when the birth order of the child is examined as a variable: children with older siblings of the opposite sex pick up more cross-gender behaviour than do those without. Here again, power may be equated with control of resources, since older children frequently have more responsibility and freedom in this than their younger siblings.

Perhaps the most obvious question that ought to

be asked is why, if gender roles are influenced by parental power, more girls do not identify with their fathers? For one thing, it has been found (not surprisingly) that children more readily imitate a model to whom they can see their own similarity. For another there is actually good evidence that girls do identify with their more powerful fathers with some persistence. Girls from about three and a half to six and a half are more heterogenous than boys: some are predominantly feminine, choosing practically all the feminine alternatives in any experimental situation, others are predominantly masculine, and some are a mixture of both. Again, from three and a half to ten and a half, boys consistently express a stronger preference for the masculine role than girls do for the feminine role; and from six to ten girls show a very strong preference for the masculine role. Thereafter the changeover is associated with the approach of puberty and with stronger pressure on girls from parents and peers to be traditionally feminine in outlook, interests, behaviour and activities.

If the mother is working and earning money, one would expect that to alter the balance of power and so affect the gender identities of the children. In fact, the daughters of working mothers have been found to score low on an index of traditional femininity. One study (edited by Nye and Hoffman) found that 'The young sons of working mothers appear to be generally more dependent; they are more obedient, less self-reliant, less sociable and more likely to seek succourance from adults. The young daughters, on the other hand, appear to be aggressive, dominant, disobedient, and independent.'

Children in families where both parents work outside the home may tend to see adult gender roles as less differentiated. This may partly result from the fact that when the wife works the husband takes a larger part in coping with the household tasks, though research suggests that this does not happen to the degree one might expect.

Power is not the only factor that encourages the close identification necessary for the learning of gender roles. Identification is also strongest when the relationship between parent and child is affectionate and warm. This holds true not only of girls, but of boys—boys acquire masculine gender roles more easily if their fathers behave affectionately towards them. A study of a group of juvenile delinquents by Andry has highlighted the fact that delinquent boys' fathers may deprive them of love—that 'paternal deprivation' of love, and hence of the relationship in which the boy can successfully learn his gender role, may be more important as a cause of male delinquency than maternal inadequacy (the factor usually blamed).

Male delinquency may be linked with other facets of the gender learning process. For instance, it has been shown that aggressive children are more often those who have been punished physically, while non-aggressive children have been disciplined by the withdrawal of love. What happens in some families is that mothers discipline girls using one technique and boys another—and that the punishment of boys is often left till the father comes home. This encourages the boy's identification with his mother rather than his father, a factor which is found in many abnormalities of male gender identity and gender role development, including the kind of 'compensatory masculinity' (the display of exaggerated masculine traits along with some feminine ones) which is frequently in the background of male juvenile delinquency.

Parents are not only individuals: they are also members of general groups; and some of the child's identification with parental models is not personal, but positional—that is, the parent is perceived as a member of distinct age, sex and status groups. This finding has emerged to explain the fact that, despite the obvious variations in the way parents behave towards their children, there is remarkable consensus among young children in their conceptions of gender roles. The conceptions of their gender roles held by middle-class and lower-class children, or by white children and negro children, suggest that they are absorbing the same cultural stereotypes, as well as imitating parental models. These stereotypes may be produced by the child even if he lacks the model (which does not mean that his development of gender identity proceeds smoothly, only that he is aware that he has to acquire a particular kind of gender role). Boys of five to seven who have been raised with their fathers absent still differentiate between mother's and father's roles on the basis of nurturance, power, aggression and competence, though they do not choose the father as the physical disciplinarian as much as boys raised with their father present. Ruth Hartley, in an article on 'Sex Role Concepts Among Elementary School Age Girls', presents data showing that children of eight to eleven maintain 'quite traditional concepts of sex-connected roles, often in conflict with their own self-definitions. Their responses to questions concerning what "most men" and "most women" do are quite different from what happens in their own primary groups. It is almost as if they discount their immediate personal experiences in favour of some impersonal criterion impinging on them from an unspecified external source.'

Children pick up their ideas about what sort of gender roles exist outside their own families partly through contact with other children and partly from their broadening social horizons in general. The books they are given to read, for instance, are full of cultural stereotypes, and reading may be a very influential source of ideas and ideals.

A series of textbooks adopted by California in 1969 for teaching children of four to eight to read (and used by something like 380,000 children in 1970) contains eighteen stories featuring the home: the woman wears an apron in twelve of them and her chief occupations are portrayed as washing dishes, cooking, sewing and ironing. Father's chief occupation is coming home. He is never seen wiping away Janet's tears and helping Mark clean his room; he plays ball with Mark. Mother never goes to work or cleans the car; she helps Janet make a cake. Mark shows Janet his toys—parachute, rocket, spacesuit,

184

helmet—and says he is an astronaut. Janet shows Mark her playhouse, chairs, dolls, and dishes: what she is is obvious and need not be put into words. Janet is given new skates and falls down when trying them for the first time: 'She is just like a girl: she gives up,' says Mark. Janet tries again. Mark says 'Now you can skate, but just with me to help you.' Thus among the many aspects of gender role transmitted by these texts are the female's greater dependency and timidity. Even in the sections featuring animal stories, Little Bear has a male pronoun and spends his time looking for fun: little Frog, with the female pronoun, sits on a rock asking people what to do.

Other textbooks demonstrate gender-role differentiation outside the home; in one, which illustrates various professions, the occupations open to women are shown as typist, secretary, school teacher, waitress and librarian. (In most textbooks it is assumed that female roles and activities are focused in the home and it is only the male who really ventures into the world outside.) One subsidiary effect of this rigid protrayal of gender roles by school textbooks is of course that they help to prevent the children developing a sense of shared human identity and potential, leading them to expect a world divided by sex and gender.

Children of five or six may be very receptive to this literature, impressed as they are by the world of school they have just entered. But their sensitivity to cultural stereotypes seems to increase still more in late childhood and is particularly acute in adolescence, which is a critical period for the development or confirmation of gender roles. Adolescence represents the transition from learning adult gender roles to performing them, and adolescent boys and girls who cannot for some reason play the appropriate gender roles are subject for the first time to real social ridicule. For boys, the relationship between physical development and gender role may become particularly acute. It is important within their own sex group, especially in athletic activities; and outside it, in contacts with the opposite sex, it takes on a new dimension with adolescence. Girls, on the other hand, find that, in the performance of their gender role, personal attractiveness is their most important asset. (The drop in the school achievement of many girls at this time is a side effect of their new concentration on personal appearance.)

As they move out into the adult world, adolescents find that the roles they are expected to fill are sharply differentiated by sex. One study shows that adults judge the adjustment of young women in terms of manners and success in marriage, while they judge the adjustment of young men in terms of performance on the job, level of aspiration, and commonsense. The parents who say that education is not important for girls are expressing the commonly held view that the female's gender role centres on domesticity, while the male's is oriented towards achievement and career, and the adolescent finds that this view is reflected in the opportunities for further education and vocational training offered to boys and girls.

So children are transformed into adults who are not only conscious of their gender roles but have, through long years of learning, internalised them and made them part of their own personalities. The process of socialisation by which this is done extends through childhood into adult life. Harriet Holter in her sociological analysis of 'Sex Roles and Social Structure' considers the early learning of gender roles only one mechanism for maintaining sex differentiation in society. Others include sanctions applied to adults (as well as children) when they deviate from their gender roles, and the sex-typed models provided by the mass media.

Sanctions usually take the form of social ridicule, though they may sometimes be enforced institutionally or even by law. There are also economic sanctions—as, for instance, in the severe problems confronting the single woman with children, whose economic difficulties are an index of society's disapproval. Sanctions, as Holter points out, are liable to emanate from many sources, since gender roles are publicly visible and most people feel competent to judge how other people fill them.

The ways in which the mass media reinforce gender roles are insidious and pervasive. The images they present reflect and exploit society's definition of gender roles. To take just one example, it is enlightening to compare Polish and American women's magazines in the early 1950s. In the American magazines the idealised woman was young, feminine, domesticated, pursuing a man, or (if she already had one) devoted to the care of home and children. The Polish stereotype showed women as economically equal with men rather than parasitic on them, as not having a different role within the family and as attracting men by their success at work. This was the official Polish ideology on the family at that time.

Children not only pick up their gender roles. They often exaggerate them. An illustration of this was the remark of a five-year-old American boy quoted by Kohlberg: 'Oh Daddy, how old will I be when I can go hunting with you? We'll go in the woods, you with your gun, me with my bow and arrow. Daddy, wouldn't it be neat if we could lasso a wild horse?' This child, reared in urban America, with an academic, distinctly non-horseriding, non-hunting father, had presumably assimilated the image of his father as a man to the image of man created by the mass media.

If children's gender roles and identities can be so clearly correlated with variations in social stereotypes and parental models, the implication is that they are very largely a product of culture—that 'gender' is indeed something quite distinct from 'sex'. Nothing should be more convincing than the mass of associations that have emerged between an individual's masculinity or femininity and socially determined norms of behaviour, attitude, expectation and role. If gender has a biological source of any kind, then culture makes it invisible. The evidence of

how people acquire their gender identities, taken

together with the facts set out in the previous chapter, suggests strongly that gender has no biological origin, that the connections between sex and gender are not really 'natural' at all.

8

The future of sex differences

On the whole, Western society is organised around the assumption that the differences between the sexes are more important than any qualities they have in common. When people try to justify this assumption in terms of 'natural' differences, two separate processes become confused: the tendency to differentiate by sex, and the tendency to differentiate in a particular way by sex. The first is genuinely a constant feature of human society but the second is not, and its inconstancy marks the division between 'sex' and 'gender': sex differences may be 'natural', but gender differences have their source in culture, not nature. Much of the confusion in the debate about sex roles comes from the fact that we tend to speak of 'sex differences' when we are really talking about differences of gender. Because of this the rationale of a society organised around sex differences is never made clear and the idea of a society based on liberation from conventional gender roles is written off as an impossibility.

The aura of naturalness and inevitability that surrounds gender-differentiation in modern society comes, then, not from biological necessity but simply from the beliefs people hold about it. In particular, most people believe that there are inborn differences between the sexes; that differentiation increases social efficiency; and that differentiation is a natural law.

The most influential of these three beliefs is the first—that gender differences mirror innate differences between the sexes. Throughout the centuries this belief has accounted for much of the passion in the debate about sex differences, and indeed it is no coincidence that, each time the debate is renewed, more or less the same sentiments are voiced as reasons for strengthening the system of gender-differentiation in places where it is being eroded by feminism.

Various techniques are used to do this, the basic being the 'gynaecological' one. One example of this is an article on 'The Potential of Women' by the gynaecologist, Edmund Overstreet, which puts forward the historically recurring view of woman as a string of endocrine glands, controlling two ovaries in charge of a uterus. Overstreet recounts the difference in hormonal secretion between the sexes, and the physiological basis of menstruation and reproduction, arguing that

6 these structural and functional differences by their very nature, produce mentational and emotional behaviour in the woman which is different from that of the man. 9

He ends:

6 When you come right down to it, perhaps women just live too long. Maybe when they get through having babies they have outlived their usefulness—especially now that they outlive men by so many years. 9

It is easy to find examples of this technique in the history of the debate over sex differences. Mary Wollstonecraft, in her introduction to the 'Vindication of the Rights of Women' (1792) quotes a comment which is the exact predecessor of Overstreet's: one writer, she says, 'asks what business women turned of forty have to do in the world.' The gynaecological technique reaches its apex in Lundberg and Farnham's 'Modern Woman: the Lost Sex', which appeared in 1947; another prime instance of it is a book entitled unequivocally 'The Biological Tragedy of Woman' published in Russia in 1930 which contains the statment:

6 By means of the nervous and endocrine systems, the ovaries through their mighty hormones hold in their power the entire organism of woman, and subject all her life processes to the dictatorship of the genius of the race. 9

Which, though dramatically worded, is essentially the same doctrine as that expressed today.

In reality, of course, as opposed to popular myth, the biological differences between the sexes are often no more significant than those between individuals. Biological variability between individuals increases the further up the evolutionary scale one goes, so that a very wide range of size and function is found in most human organs, tissues and secretions.

The female clitoris and male penis vary enormously in size, and so do the stomach, the oesophagus, the duodenum, the colon, the liver, the bladder, the heart and the heart rate, the distribution of muscle and fat, the chemical make-up of blood and saliva, the weight and shape of the thyroid gland, and so on. Sometimes the range of difference is not just 50% or 100% but 10 or 50 fold. For example, the size of normal ovaries varies from 2 grams to 10 grams; normal heart rates of normal males range from 45 to 105 beats per minute, and the heart's pumping capacity may be normally 3.16 litres of blood per minute or 10.81. On all these measures females vary as much as males, so a significant proportion of males and females are in the same group with respect to size, height, heart rate and hormone levels, to name a few of the parameters. Even in the form of the external genitals there is a range extending from very female to very male, and it is along this range that all individuals, male and female, normal and abnormal, fall. One expert on intersexuality has said that it is impossible to define male and female genital morphologies as distinct: they exist as a continuum of possible developments and are thus a constant reminder, not of the biological polarity of male and female, but of their biological identity.

The same is true of the evidence (referred to in Chapter 1) that there may be differences in the hormonal sensitivity of the central nervous system in men and women. If this does indeed occur it would not create two distinct types—male and female—but a whole range from very male to very female over which individuals would be distributed as they are for other variables. Further, whatever the outcome of this research may be, it does not absolve us from certain critical social choices: these choices are distinctively human and no amount of animal experimentation will determine which way our choice has to go.

The argument for the 'social efficiency' of our present gender roles centres round woman's place as housewife and mother. There is also the more vaguely conceived belief that any tampering with these roles would diminish happiness, but this type of argument has a blatantly disreputable history and should have been discarded long ago. 'Happiness' can be a cover-term for conservatism, and countless evils can be sanctioned in the name of some supposed short-term psychic gain. The most famous historical example is the subjection of negroes to slavery. It is frequently said that too much equality, too little differentiation, threatens the success of marriage. Only if the sexes are complementary (that is, differentiated) can the intense emotional relationship of modern marriage survive. In effect this means that the simple distinction between male and female is elaborated into one between masculine and feminine, with husband and wife differing in their power, their ability to take decisions, their relations with the world outside the home, their leisure interests, and so on. It is now considered all right for wives to work outside the home, but only if they do not compete with their husbands for success in their careers or for earning power: marriage manuals advise working wives to be careful to preserve the traditional balance of power in the home, so as not to 'demasculinise' their husbands (and 'defeminise' themselves).

This aspect of gender role differentiation is liable to prove the most difficult of all to change. In the USSR, where the emancipation of women has been approaching the point where women—and to some extent men too—are liberated from their traditional gender roles, women still keep their two roles at work and at home. Cheap or free child care by the state kindergartens does not take from women the responsibility for maintaining the home, preparing the family's food, caring for the family's clothes, or even caring for the child when the child is at home.

Road mending in Moscow   (Paul Popper)

Throughout our society, permeating popular literature and the mass media generally, one finds an insistence on the importance of the mother-child tie. Mothering is held to be the principal foundation of the adult's security, psychological health, and social adjustment. The importance of motherhood is seen not as something biological—a matter of giving birth or providing milk—but as social and psychological. Social norms persuade mothers (and fathers) that the mother's duty to the child is constant attendance throughout childhood, and a particularly heightened sensitivity to its needs during the early months. This is not the finding of research, but a distortion of the general conclusion researchers have come to. Infants do need not only good physical care but warm and intimate relationships with others; they need a certain minimum of continuity in the people caring for them, and they need both verbal and nonverbal stimulation. But no researcher has ever found that they must have these needs satisfied by mothers rather than fathers, by females rather than males, or indeed by adults rather than older siblings. Of course, a culture that develops tenderness and sympathy only in women may have a considerable need for the mother-child tie.

With child care made into a purely feminine task, it is particularly important that women should be well prepared for motherhood and well adjusted to it. This is why we have all the mechanisms for creating and maintaining sex differentiation prior to adulthood, from the femininity of the nursing and teaching professions to doll play.

Dolls are not found much in small-scale societies, but they are universal in highly civilised ones, where they allow girls to rehearse their role as mothers throughout childhood. Actually many females spend more time with their dolls then they do with their babies, a fact which underlines how much successful maternity depends on successful learning. Animal studies confirm that: maternal behaviour is not primarily a function of gestation or hormonal balance but of proximity with the young, and one can get

(Pictorial Press)

most mammals, male or female, virgin or nonvirgin, to behave maternally by caging them with young. Spontaneous 'maternal' infant care is not universally a female activity in all species: in some it is male, and in some it is common to both sexes, as it can be in human society. When Margaret Mead presented dolls to Manus children for the first time, it was the boys who took them up and played with them, not the girls; maternity was more congruent with the masculine gender role there than it was with the feminine. Harry Harlow's famous paper 'On the Nature of Love', based on his experiments with monkeys, came to the conclusion that the maternal feature infant monkeys respond to is not milk or femaleness, or the smell of their biological mother, but fur—that is, body contact. Perhaps this is what mothers in all species learn to offer.

A mother's encouragement of doll play in childhood symbolises real maternity to a child, and mothers are certainly all-important as role models for their daughters: bad mothers produce daughters who make bad mothers in turn—amongst humans as well as other primates. Monkey mothers who have not learned motherhood tread on their babies with careless nonchalance; human mothers unprepared for motherhood may end up as a statistic under the heading 'battered baby syndrome'.

No one, then, would deny the need for warmth and love in motherhood: what is at issue is not the degree of maternal care but the exclusiveness of it—the assumption that fathers need not (perhaps cannot) share to anything like the same extent in a vital part of their children's upbringing. This belief has nothing to do with the inborn nature of human beings: it stems primarily from the fact that the economic organisation of our society does not allow the father to be present in the home for much of the time.

Perhaps it is not too far fetched to attribute some of the (male) expert's preoccupation with the psychological significance of motherhood to both (male) guilt over the consigning of child care to females and (male) envy of the female procreative function. Kate Millett might find this a respectable hypothesis, but so also do the psychoanalysts Bruno Bettelheim and Peter Lomas. The former has written an extensive account of rituals symbolising male womb envy in preliterate societies; the latter, in a notable but ignored article some years ago, suggested that the medical treatment of childbirth in our society reeks of dehumanisation (of the mother) which is in turn related to the male's envy of female creative achievement in childbirth. The practice of episiotomy (a cut in the perineum before or during the birth process to facilitate the actual birth) which is universal in some maternity hospitals, is not very far removed from the category of 'symbolic wounds' discussed by Bettelheim, and perhaps even more significant for its perpetration by male upon female rather than by male upon male.

The assumption that a woman's place is in the home implies that it is not in a career. When women do take outside jobs they find, as we have already seen, that their work is almost always traditional 'feminine work' conforming to conventional ideas of gender roles.

In factories, a division of labour between the sexes is invariably maintained, supported by references to 'natural' differences between the sexes and to the economic efficiency that would be lost if the work roles of men and women were interchangeable. Men will not work under women because 'women make bad foremen'—they have the wrong kind of temperament and, in any case, men do not like being ordered around by women. Hence any deviation on the factory floor from the rule of male-superior female-inferior produces industrial unrest and the possibility of lower production.

Research into the attitudes of Norwegian and Swedish employers, for example, has revealed that women are placed in unskilled, routine and closely supervised factory jobs because they are considered more suited to these than to jobs requiring skill and autonomy. The employers justify their policy by remarking that the women concerned easily accept the repetitiveness, lack of opportunity for advancement and lack of independence that is associated with such work. Similarly, women make better nurses because they have the 'nursing disposition' that men lack. Secretaries are females because of their 'feminine' characteristics—they are more cooperative and accept supervision more readily than men. Women sell goods in department stores because 'female characteristics' are best—'gentleness' and the 'ability to adjust'.

This kind of reasoning is used to extend sex differentiation into new spheres as well as to maintain it in those where it already exists. The Swedish study, for instance, showed a tendency for employers to class industrial occupations as feminine if they could be associated with traditional female work, such as cooking, sewing and nursing: in the electrical industry winding work was labelled as feminine because of its resemblance to sewing.

This kind of extension of 'feminine' activities is, of course, based on the way we live, in families. The asymmetrical structure of the family—father at work, mother at home—allows a connection to be made between such diverse activities as the feeding of tiny babies, the cleaning of houses, and the washing of dirty socks. In reality, while childbearing is a biological function, and therefore female, domestic work is a social/economic one, and therefore sexually neuter; but where both are in practice feminine, the biological role of motherhood takes on a whole aura of domesticity and cultural femininity. The lines are tied between the act of giving birth and the act of cleaning the house, and the status of women as a group is coloured by these secondary cultural consequences of the primary biological specialisation. From that point on, it is not biology that determines the role of women, but domesticity.

How this state of affairs came about is a complicated process, but the industrial revolution was certainly a prime agent in creating the division between home and work-place. It is this division which is advanced as an enduring reason for sex differentiation now—for instance, in the discriminatory attitude of employers which is based, very realistically, on the fact that women run the home while men do not. In fact this is blamed for more than its fair share of evils. Absenteeism is higher among women than men, but not because of their domestic responsibilities. Careful tabulation has revealed that it is highly correlated with education (though why is not known) and that it is sex differences in education that account for the differences in absenteeism. This is a good example of how feminine personality ('women are not so reliable, they only work for pin money') is blamed for something which results from cultural deprivation.

Even where women's position at work is apparently being protected, the result can still be to increase the discrimination against them. In all industrialised countries there is legislation which commonly limits the hours women may work, the weights they may lift and the jobs they make take on. In one American state the weight limit is fifteen pounds—a weight exceeded by a three-month-old baby. While such legislation exists—as it does on a wide scale—it severely limits the opportunities for women to get jobs offering equal pay, prospects, training and so on. For instance the 1964 United States Civil Rights Act has been held by judicial decision not to nullify any of the restrictions imposed on women by the protective labour legislation. This has made women, as one Californian Justice put it, 'victims of their own protection'. The 1963 Equal Pay Act only overrides protective legislation when male and female are engaged on 'similar' work. Where the work is 'dissimilar' a wage-differential is allowable. But work is dissimilar when male and female lift different weights, for example, which they do because of the protective labour legislation; hence the Equal Pay Act does not apply. Case law demonstrates that this is a trap from which no one can escape, least of all the employers, who anyway do not want to because it is in their advantage to exploit it.

Protective labour legislation, and the doctrine underlying it, offer a ready opportunity for the extension of sex differentiation to other spheres. The doctrine of 'separate but equal' has been derived from the legal doctrine that 'sex is a valid basis for classification' and used to uphold many discriminations, including the exclusion of women from educational institutions and, as recently as 1966, from juries.

Gender-differentiation persists, then, in industrial society, basically because of the importance people continue to attach to masculinity and femininity. They see a whole mass of distinctions between male and female as necessary to social life. But is our form of gender-differentiation actually related to any goal of social or economic efficiency? Moreover, do men and women like being 'masculine' and 'feminine': are they happy in their gender identities? What difference does sex make? What difference should it make?

In answering these questions, some facts about our own industrial society should be borne in mind. (1) The average woman has between two and three children, and there is a population problem of immense proportions on the horizon. (2) The majority of mothers do not breast-feed their babies—that is, they choose not to. There has been a 30-40% drop in the incidence of breast-feeding in many countries over recent decades, and something like 70-80% of all babies in industrialised cultures are weaned from the breast by the time they leave the maternity hospital. (3) The life span of women is now about seventy-five years, of which probably less than two or three years is spent in a state of pregnancy or lactation. The average woman spends about 6% of her fertile years—or about 3% or her total life span—bound by the reproductive tie. (4) There are no known medical reasons (despite a great deal of research) why pregnancy should interfere with a woman's other activities, whatever these are, for the sake of her health or that of the child. Even assuming that a woman withdraws from other activity during pregnancy and lactation, about 97% of her lifetime remains.

In political life, as in industry, popular beliefs about sexual equality contrast with the realities of discrimination. Democratic ideology proposes political participation as a sine qua non of equality, and popular myth has it that the political roles of men and women are less distinct than they used to be—that the granting of the suffrage to women was, and continues to be, an automatic guarantee of political equality. This is very far from the truth. Again, egalitarian ideology conceals the presence of a basic, and at times insidious, differentiation, which will militate against equality so long as—and perhaps longer than—it goes unrecognised.

Even in their use of the suffrage, men and women differ; in most countries where women have the vote, significantly more women than men tend to be non-voters. Duverger, in his study of 'The Political Role of Women' found female non-voters exceeding males sometimes by as much as 24%, though a figure of 10% was more typical. Duverger's data may be a little out of date now (he collected it in the early 1950s) but the trend he discerned towards increasing *inequality* between male and female in political life is now well-established. His diagrammatic representation of the political roles of the sexes (see Figure 7) is therefore of continuing relevance. Moreover, this political inequality extends to communist countries, where there has been much more of a deliberate effort to reduce the political gap.

Even when women do achieve political office, they do so in a context of male predominance, and the historical trend is, again, not an egalitarian one. In 1951 4% of the French parliament was female, and by 1967 the proportion had dropped to 2.3%. At that time, women accounted for 4.1% of the British Parliament and in the United States (supposedly a matriarchal society) for only 2.5% of the House of Representatives. Where the number of women in

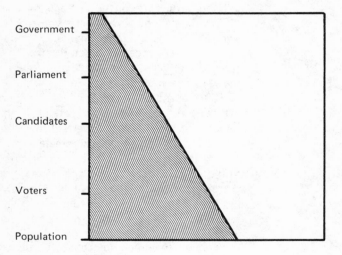

7 Political roles of men and women. (The proportion of women to men at the various levels is shown by the proportion of shaded to white space.)

politics has increased, the increase has been at lower levels—in municipal government—parallel with the tendency shown in Duverger's diagram.

Once in political office, men and women seem to reflect, in an extremely persistent fashion, the roles of non-political life. Women concentrate on public health and 'family' questions, on education, children, and women's rights, while men specialise in finance, economics, the administration of internal policy, agriculture, national defence, and foreign affairs, thus directing all the affairs of the nation which (in the narrow sense of the word) are not domestic.

Looking at all these ways in which our practice of gender differentiation contradicts our ideology, it is noticeable that, while small-scale societies often have less gender-differentiation in practice than they do in theory, we seem to have reversed the order. This is odd. Societies lacking in technology are more bound in every way by the reproductive specialisation of male and female. When anthropologists say that sex is a criterion for the ascription of tasks and roles in all known societies, they are stating the obvious for social groups still organised on a small-scale ('primitive') basis. Pregnancy is a socially visible and physically obvious fact, whatever the extent of its supposed limitations on women's activities. Human lactation is often the only source of milk for infants, and, continuing for perhaps two or three years for each surviving child, creates a further sex distinction by dividing a society into lactating and non-lactating groups. High rates of mortality among foetuses and infants mean more pregnancy per woman per surviving child than in medically sophisticated societies. The total effect of all this is to build a structure of sex differentiation which has nothing to do with personality, intellect, or sexuality as such, but a great deal to do with the survival tasks of the society in question.

If our own society is largely independent of these constraints, its organisation of gender roles around the division of work and home does have a certain function. As femininists have not been slow to point out, it guarantees the servicing of the (predominantly male) industrial work force by the (predominantly female) domestic work force. Further, it provides society with an army of consumers—housewives—whose economically unproductive role has been essential to the success of Western capitalism. (This does not mean that society could not be equally well organised in another way: the Swedish economist Holmberg maintains that the elimination of sex differentiation would increase national productivity considerably, despite the financial costs of retraining and reorganisation that would be involved.)

But in the end it is not the argument from social efficiency that keeps gender roles in being; it is the simple belief that a society without gender differentiation is somehow wrong in itself. Comments on the appearance and dress of today's youth often hinge on some statement like 'You can't tell the boys from the girls any more.' This may be true, but is it true that boys and girls must be distinguishable in dress and appearance? Does it matter if they look the same? The answer is a tautological one: we believe that girls and boys should look different because we feel they ought to (and we feel uncomfortable if they do not).

This mechanism of belief sustains gender-differentiation just as a similar mechanism sustains differences of caste. Gender, like caste, is a matter of social ascription which bears no necessary relation to the individual's own attributes and inherent abilities. In this sense, gender and 'caste' are sociologically identical, and the capacity of caste to survive change is shared by gender.

Indeed, far from differentiation by gender having decreased in recent years, it has in many ways intensified, making the belief that innate sex differences justify differences of gender role something of a self-fulfilling prophecy. While employers, amongst others, continue to insist that temperamental differences between the sexes fit them for different work-roles, two consequences are guaranteed: firstly, the differentiation of work-roles

The Isle
of Wight
1970
(Paul
Popper)

by gender will persist, and secondly, the belief that there are innate sex differences in temperament will appear to be vindicated.

Differentiation of work-roles by gender is a remarkably constant feature throughout industrial society generally (see Chapter 5) and its persistence is particularly notable in countries like Sweden where concerted efforts have been made to break it down. Some things seem to be highly unresponsive to political action, and employers' attitudes to female labour are a case in point.

It is perhaps surprising that gender differentiation should be so strong and so persistent in countries like Scandinavia and Britain with a predominantly egalitarian ideology. Research shows that individual people who hold egalitarian beliefs are more likely to view men and women as being similarly endowed. On the other hand, there is a disparity between belief and practice. A Norwegian psychologist who asked mothers whether or not they discriminated in their treatment of boys and girls, found that the majority gave egalitarian answers: but when asked about *specific* practices the mothers showed that they had a marked tendency to act out traditional norms.

An official and institutional commitment to egalitarianism may lead people to believe they *are* equal, so focussing even feminists' attention on minor discrepancies in the legal treatment of women, rather than on major discrepancies between this and the private, informal stress on the importance of sex differences, such as one may find in the family. Changes in sex roles, such as the growing proportion of women in employment, are taken to prove that sex differentiation is lessening, despite the evidence that women are still confined to certain types of work.

The existence of institutional opportunities for sex equality is misleading in another way, in that there is considerable evidence that many of them are not taken up because women fear the loss of their femininity. Higher education is one example: the technical specialisations are theoretically open to women but very few in fact choose them.

This seemingly regressive trend faced Duverger in his study of women in politics, and caused him to ask why women should agree to specialise in family, household, and educational matters, and why they were not more 'feminist'. Using evidence of the ways in which political roles are differentiated by gender in four countries (Germany, Norway, France and Yugoslavia) he described the traditional world of the female as closed, limited and introvertive: as inimical to the development of the general, macrocosmic, and relatively impersonal interests that politics requires. Thus he said 'femininity' and politics are opposed, because politics has traditionally been a man's world, and women's roles in the home have tied them to certain confined interests and circumscribed ways of life. He expected that as the employment of women increased, so would women's participation in politics: since this has not happened one must conclude that employment does not encourage political awareness and activity so much as domesticity has impeded it—and will apparently continue to impede it.

Both the way in which women are enveloped by domestic responsibility and the way in which their political role is not substantial enough for true egalitarianism, suggest that it may be the family which insists on traditional gender-role differentiation in a more deterministic fashion than any other social or economic force. The family as it has evolved in industrial societies is a triad of inequality and difference, perhaps the least democratic of contemporary institutions, and in this sense a potent dictator of inequality elsewhere.

At the present time, society is becoming oriented around the nuclear family, and this means that gender identity has to be acquired more and more narrowly within the family. In turn, disorders of the identification process become more likely, and these produce personality disorders which may contribute to the rising figures for mental illness.

Speculation of this kind can be carried on in the same vein ad infinitum. Studies of the way sex roles have changed in recent years show that they have undergone no radical reversal. Most changes (such as the increasing employment of women) have been superficial, failing to affect the traditional balance of relationships between the sexes and the traditional definitions of gender roles. Ruth Hartley, studying the concept of sex roles held by girls, has suggested that many of the difficulties in the current social scene may be due to the *lack* of change in these concepts—that is, to a lack of adjustment to a changed and changing reality—rather than to the confusion which many people have seen as a consequence of women's emancipation. Most working mothers tell their daugthers they work for the money, whereas they tell social scientists they work because they like to work. Hence daughters grow up believing that the only justifiable reason for a mother to work outside the home is financial need. When they reach motherhood themselves, they may discover what their mothers discovered—that although motherhood is expected to be a full-time occupation for adult women, the satisfactions of rearing children do not entirely counterbalance the physical isolation of the mother in the home, or the endlessly repetitive routine of housework. They then have to work out for themselves, as their mothers did, all the problems of guilt and anxiety which research shows to be the only difference between working mothers and non-working mothers on all indices of maternal adequacy and personal adjustment.

Most of the debate about sex differences is angled at proving that women are, or are not, different from men, rather than proving that men are or are not different from women. If this fact needs explaining, it is enough to point out that the bias of our culture is still patriarchal; it is women who are claiming the rights of men and who need to be defended against charges of inferiority. Perhaps there is only one area in which attempts are made to prove the reverse—that men are not inferior to women—and that is the home. But even the most participatory father is not shamed by either real or imputed failure, since he retains the prestige of his masculinity, and indeed it is in terms of this masculinity that his inability to care sensitively and tirelessly for small children is explained.

Though the emphasis is on the condition of womanhood, the roles of both sexes are under scrutiny, and if women suffer from their status as second-class citizens, men certainly suffer from the exercise of privilege. The strains of playing the masculine role in modern civilisation show signs of mounting to breaking point. Social stress diseases are killing proportionately far more males now than they were at the beginning of the century. In 1900 about 177 males in 100,000 died of heart diseases in the United States and 159 females; in 1953 the figures were 382 and 225. Ulcers of the stomach and duodenum were responsible for 3.2 male deaths per 100,000 male population in 1900, and 8.6 in 1953; the figures for females were 3.0 and 1.9. For ulcers, the male rate has more than doubled, while the female rate has actually declined. Whereas the major cause of death in 1900 in the West used to be infectious illness (pneumonia, influenza, gastroenteritis, tuberculosis) heart disease is now the prime killer.

One cannot prove that current gender roles are unsatisfactory on a personal level: one can only point at obvious strains that are in some way related to them—at the fact that the conventional woman's role does not include achievement as an ideal and women tend to withdraw from the possibility of achievement, while the man's role is built around it and men seem particularly vulnerable to illnesses caused by 'social stress'.

Seeing sex differentiation as a natural fact of life, as many people do, diverts our attention from the strangely inconsequential fact that our society, having achieved most of the equipment and knowledge necessary to dispense with sex differentiation everywhere except in the bedroom and the maternity hospital, nevertheless maintains it as a near-universal feature of the social structure. The invention of highly sophisticated machinery relieving work of its physical burden has not weakened sex differentiation in industry: the artificial feeding of infants has not liberated women any more than it has domesticated men. Perhaps, as some have suggested, it is a condition of civilisation that men should be excluded from the care of the next generation and from all the qualities and habits associated with maternity; but what kind of civilisation is this? If it is a civilisation that encourages three-year-old boys to fight back, that disciplines them with the hand rather than with the word, precisely in order that they should become strong, punitive, aggressive men in their turn, then the political machinations which lead to war have their beginning in the nursery, and neither men nor women can expect men to stop fighting wars until the experience of the small boy teaches him to value love and tenderness, non-violence and the urge to protect, instead of the will to destroy, and to see these as human, rather than feminine, qualities. If it is a civilisation that gives dolls to female children so they can have practice at mothering, it is a civilisation that teaches girls to expect their greatest achievements to be maternal ones, to repress and inhibit the development of all their other capacities, so that their maternal destinies can be fulfilled in a world which is already over-populated and able to offer them, at best, less than a decade of active maternity.

While our society is organised around the differences rather than the similarities between the sexes, these two extremes of masculinity and femininity will recur, so apparently confirming the belief that they come from a biological cause. Whatever biological cause there is in reality, however influential or insubstantial it may be, thus tends to become increasingly irrelevant and the distorted view of its importance becomes increasingly a rationalisation of what is, in fact, only prejudice. In this matter, human beings are probably more conditioned by their own gender-differentiated upbringing than they are able, or would care, to admit.

References and further reading

References and further reading

CHAPTER 1

M E Backett 'Domestic Accidents' Public Health Papers 26 W H O Geneva, 1965

F E Check 'A Serendipitous Finding: Sex Roles and Schizophrenia' Journal of Abnormal and Social Psychology 1964, vol 69, no 4, p 392-400

F A E Crew 'Sex Determination' Methuen, 1965

K Dalton 'The Menstrual Cycle' Penguin, 1969

M Diamond (ed) 'Perspectives in Reproduction and Sexual Behaviour' Indiana University Press, 1968

J W B Douglas and J M Blomfield 'Children Under Five' Allen & Unwin, 1958

G M Gilbert 'A Survey of Referral Problems in Metropolitan Child Guidance Centers' Journal of Clinical Psychology 1957, 13, p 37-40

G Gorer 'Bali and Angkor' Michael Joseph, 1936

R Greene 'Human Hormones' World University Library, Weidenfeld, 1970

D A Hamburg and D T Lunde 'Sex Hormones in the Development of Sex Differences' in E E Maccoby (ed) 'The Development of Sex Differences' Tavistock Publications, 1967

G A Harrison, J S Weiner, J M Tanner and N A Barnicot 'Human Biology' Clarendon Press, 1968

R B Hersey 'Emotional Cycles in Man' Asylum: Journal of Mental Science 1931, 77, 151,

The Lancet 'The Physiological Basis of Aggression' leader article 15 Nov 1969, p 1052-3

R LeVine (ed) 'Endocrines and the Central Nervous System' Proceedings of the Association for Research in Nervous and Mental Disease, Williams and Wilkins, 1966

S LeVine 'Sex Differences in the Brain' Scientific American April 1966, vol 214, no 4

W H Masters and J W Ballew 'The Third Sex' Geriatrics Jan 1955, vol 10, no 1, p 1-4

J Money 'Developmental Differentiation of Femininity and Masculinity Compared' in S M Farber and R H L Wilson (eds) 'The Potential of Woman' Man and Civilisation Symposium, McGraw-Hill, 1963

J Money (ed) 'Psychosexual Differentiation' in 'Sex Research: New Developments' Holt, Rinehart & Winston, 1965

J Money 'Sex Hormones and Other Variables in Human Eroticism' in W C Young (ed) 'Sex and Internal Secretions' Bailliere, Tindall & Cox, 1961

A Montagu 'The Natural Superiority of Woman' Macmillan, New York, 1968

C Overzier 'Intersexuality' Academic Press, 1963

'The Registrar-General's Statistical Review of England and Wales for 1969'

A M Rose (ed) 'Mental Health and Mental Disorder' Routledge, 1956

R J Schlegel and J A Bellanti 'Increased Susceptibility of Males to Infection' The Lancet 18 Oct 1969, p 826-7

E Stengel 'Suicide and Attempted Suicide' Penguin, 1964

S M Watkins 'Rival to the Witch Doctor' The Lancet 22 May 1971, p 1062-3

I B Weiner 'Psychological Disturbance in Adolescence' John Wiley, 1970

R J Williams 'Biochemical Individuality' John Wiley, 1956

CHAPTER 2

E Albert 'The Roles of Women' in S M Farber and R H L Wilson (eds) 'The Potential of Woman' Man and Civilisation Symposium, McGraw-Hill, 1963

M Amir 'Forcible Rape' in M E Wolfgang et al (ed) 'The Sociology of Crime and Delinquency' John Wiley, 1970

A Anastasi 'Differential Psychology' Macmillan, New York, 1958

H Barry, M K Bacon and I L Child 'A Cross-cultural Survey of Some Sex Differences in Socialisation' Journal of Abnormal and Social Psychology 1957, 55, p 327-32

E M Bennett and L R Cohen 'Men and Women: Personality Patterns and Contrasts' Genetic Psychology Monographs 1959, 59, p 101-155

H A Bloch and G Geis 'Man, Crime and Society' Random House, 1962

A K Cohen 'Delinquent Boys: the Culture of the Gang' Routledge, 1956

R D'Andrade 'Sex Differences and Cultural Institutions' in E E Maccoby (ed) 'The Development of Sex Differences' Tavistock Publications, 1967

W Davenport 'Sexual Patterns and their Regulation in a Society of the Southwest Pacific' in F A Beach (ed) 'Sex and Behaviour' John Wiley, 1965

L A DeLucia 'The Toy Preference Test: A Measure of Sex Role Identification' Child Development 1963, 34, p 107-117

A Gesell et al 'The First Five Years of Life' Harper, 1940

T C N Gibbens and J Prince 'Shoplifting' The Institute for the Study and Treatment of Delinquency, 1962

M Gold 'Undetected Delinquent Behaviour' in M E Wolfgang et al (ed) 'The Sociology of Crime and Delinquency' John Wiley, 1970

H Hacker 'Women as a Minority Group' Social Forces, 1951, p 60-69

E T Hall 'The Silent Language' Doubleday, 1959

H F Harlow 'Sexual Behaviour in the Rhesus Monkey' in F A Beach (ed) 'Sex and Behaviour' John Wiley, 1965

L A Hattwick 'Sex Differences in the Behaviour of Nursery School Children' Child Development Dec 1937, vol 8, no 4

F Heidensohn 'The Deviance of Women' British Journal of Sociology June 1968, Vol XIX, no 2

J Henry 'Jungle People' Vintage Books, 1964

P Kaberry 'Women of the Grassfields' HMSO, 1952

J Kagan and H A Moss 'Birth to Maturity' John Wiley, 1962

S Leith-Ross 'African Women' Faber, 1939

R A LeVine 'Sex Roles and Economic Change in Africa' Ethnology April 1966, vol V, no 2

F H McClintock and N H Avison 'Crime in England and Wales' Heinemann, 1968

M Mead 'Male and Female' Penguin, 1950

M Mead 'Sex and Temperament in Three Primitive Societies' William Morrow, 1935

L Minturn and W W Lambert 'Mothers of Six Cultures: Antecedents of Child

Rearing' John Wiley, 1964

J Money 'The Developmental Differentiation of Femininity and Masculinity Compared' in S M Farber and R H L Wilson (eds) 'The Potential of Woman' Man and Civilisation Symposium, McGraw-Hill, 1963

C E Osgood 'The Nature and Measurement of Meaning' Psychological Bulletin 1952, 49, p 197-237

O Pollak 'The Criminality of Women' University of Pennsylvania Press, 1950

S M Robinson 'Juvenile Delinquency: Its Nature and Control' Holt, 1960

H R Schaffer and P E Emerson 'Patterns of Response to Physical Contact in Early Human Development' Journal of Child Psychology and Psychiatry 1964, 5, p 1-13

R E Sears, E E Maccoby and H Levin 'Patterns of Child Rearing' Harper & Row, 1957

L M Terman and C C Miles 'Sex and Personality' McGraw-Hill, 1936

G M Weller and R Q Bell 'Basal Skin Conductance and Neonatal State' Child Development 1965, 36, p 647-57

B B Whiting (ed) 'Six Cultures: Studies of Child Rearing' John Wiley, 1963

M E Wolfgang et al 'The Sociology of Crime and Delinquency' John Wiley, 1970

CHAPTER 3

A Anastasi 'Differential Psychology' Macmillan, New York, 1958

N Bayley and E S Schaeffer 'Correlations of Maternal and Child Behaviours with the Development of Mental Abilities: data from the Berkeley Growth Study' Social Research Child Development Monograph 1964, 29, no 6, p 3-79

D Brody 'Twin Resemblances in Mechanical Ability' Child Development Sept 1937, vol 8, no 3

E Erikson 'Inner and Outer Space: Reflections on Womanhood' in R J Lifton (ed) 'The Woman in America' Houghton Mifflin, 1965

A Gesell et al 'The First Five Years of Life' Harper, 1940

J Joyce 'A Research Note on Attitudes to Work and Marriage of Six Hundred Adolescent Girls' British Journal of Sociology 1961, vol 12, p 176-83

M Komarovsky 'Cultural Contradictions and Sex Roles' American Journal of Sociology Nov 1946

D M Levy 'Maternal Overprotection' Columbia University Press, 1943

D B Lynn 'Sex Role and Parental Identification' Child Development 1962, 33, p 555-64

E E Maccoby 'Woman's Intellect' in S M Farber and R H L Wilson (eds) 'The Potential of Woman' Man and Civilisation Symposium, McGraw-Hill, 1963

E E Maccoby (ed) 'Sex Differences in Intellectual Functioning' in 'The Development of Sex Differences' Tavistock Publications, 1967

E M Plank and R Plank 'Emotional Components in Arithmetical Learning as Seen Through Autobiographies' in R S Eissler et al (eds) 'The Psychoanalytic Study of the Child' 1954, vol IX, p 274-93 International Universities Press

C I Sandstrom 'The Psychology of Childhood and Adolescence' (especially Chapters 8 & 9) Penguin, 1966

A Schoeppe 'Sex Differences in Adolescent Socialisation' Journal of Social Psychology 1953, 38, p 175-85

J Shaffer 'A Specific Cognitive Defect Observed in Gonadal Aplasia' Journal of Clinical Psychology 1962, 18, p 403-6

P Wallin 'Cultural Contradictions and Sex Roles: A Repeat Study' American Sociological Review 1950, 15, p 288-93

H A Witkin et al 'Psychological Differentiation' John Wiley, 1962

CHAPTER 4

G Bateson 'Sex and Culture' Annals of New York Academy of Science May 1947, vol XLVII

E M Brecher 'The Sex Researchers' Deutsch, 1970

A K Cohen 'Delinquent Boys: the Culture of the Gang' Routledge, 1956

K M Colby 'Sex Differences in Dreams of Primitive Tribes' American Anthropologist 1963, 65, p 1116-121

J Cowie, V Cowie and E Slater 'Delinquency in Girls' Heinemann, 1968

W Davenport 'Sexual Patterns and their Regulation in a Society of the Southwest Pacific' in F A Beach (ed) 'Sex and Behaviour' John Wiley, 1965

K Davis 'Factors in the Sex Life of 2200 Women' Harper, 1929

G Devereux 'Institutionalised Homosexuality of the Mohave Indians' Human Biology 1937, vol 9

E Figes 'Patriarchal Attitudes: Women in Society' Faber, 1970

C S Ford and F A Beach 'Patterns of Sexual Behaviour' Eyre & Spottiswode, 1952

S Freud 'Three Essays on the Theory of Sexuality' Hogarth Press, 1962

S Freud 'Femininity' in 'New Introductory Lectures on Psychoanalysis' vol XXII Hogarth Press, 1964

S Freud 'Female Sexuality' in 'Collected Papers' vol V, Hogarth Press, 1950

J H Gagnon and W Simon (eds) 'Sexual Deviance' Harper, 1967

P H Gebhard, J Raboch and H Geise 'The Sexuality of Women' Deutsch, 1970

K Horney 'Feminine Psychology' Routledge, 1967

P C Jay 'The Female Primate' in S M Farber and R H L Wilson (eds) 'The Potential of Woman' McGraw-Hill, 1963

A C Kinsey et al 'Sexual Behaviour in the Human Female' W B Saunders Company, 1953

A C Kinsey et al 'Sexual Behaviour in the Human Male' W B Saunders Company, 1949

B Malinowski 'The Sexual Life of Savages' Routledge, 1932

A H Maslow 'Self-Esteem (Dominance-Feeling) and Sexuality in Women' Journal of Social Psychology 1942, 16

W H Masters and V E Johnson 'The Sexual Response Cycles of the Human Male and Female: Comparative Anatomy and Physiology' in F A Beach (ed) 'Sex and Behaviour' John Wiley, 1965

W H Masters and V E Johnson 'Human Sexual Response' Little, Brown, 1966

M Mead 'Sex and Temperament in Three Primitive Societies' William Morrow, 1935

M Mead 'Male and Female' Penguin, 1950

M Mead 'Cultural Determinants of Sexual Behaviour' in W C Young (ed) 'Sex and Internal Secretions' Bailliere, Tindall and Cox, 1961, p 1433-79

K Millett 'Sexual Politics' Hart-Davis, 1971

J Money 'Sex Hormones and Other Variables in Human Eroticism' in W C Young (ed) 'Sex and Internal Secretions' Bailliere, Tindall and Cox, 1961, p

1383-1401

B J Oliver 'Sexual Deviation in American Society' New Haven College and University Press, 1967

G Rattray Taylor 'Sex in History' Thames & Hudson, 1953

R V Sampson 'The Psychology of Power' Pantheon, 1965

M Schofield 'The Sexual Behaviour of Young People' Penguin, 1968

D J West 'Homosexuality' Penguin, 1968

CHAPTER 5

M Ainsworth et al 'Deprivation of Maternal Care: A Reassessment of its Effects' Schocken Books, 1966 (in the same volume as Maternal Care and Mental Health by John Bowlby)

E Boserup 'Woman's Role in Economic Development' Allen & Unwin, 1970

A J Coale et al 'Aspects of the Analysis of Family Structure' Princeton University Press, 1965

R D'Andrade 'Sex Differences and Cultural Institutions' in E E Maccoby (ed) 'The Development of Sex Differences' Tavistock Publications, 1967

C Du Bois 'The People of Alor' University of Minnesota Press, 1944

E E Evans-Pritchard 'The Comparative Method in Social Anthropology' (L T Hobhouse Memorial Trust Lecture no 33) Athlone Press, 1963

E Faulkner Baker 'Technology and Woman's Work' Columbia University Press, 1964

M Fogarty et al 'Women in Top Jobs' Political and Economic Planning, Allen & Unwin, 1971

C S Ford 'A Comparative Study of Human Reproduction' Yale University Press, 1945

H Gavron 'The Captive Wife' Penguin, 1966

H Granquist 'Birth and Childhood Among the Arabs' Helsingfors, 1947

M J Herskovits 'Dahomey: An Ancient West African Kingdom' Northwestern University Press, 1967

A Hunt 'A Survey of Woman's Employment' (Government Social Survey) HMSO, 1968

R Illsley 'The Sociological Study of Reproduction and Its Outcome' in S A Richardson and A F Guttmacher (eds) 'Childbearing—its Social and Psychological Aspects' Williams and Wilkins, 1967

P Kaberry 'Women of the Grassfields' HMSO, 1952

V Klein 'Working Wives' Institute of Personnel Management

V Klein 'Women Workers' OECD, Paris, 1965

O Klineberg 'Social Psychology' Holt, 1954 (revised)

J Laffin 'Women in Battle' Abelard-Schuman, 1967

C Lévi-Strauss 'The Family' in H L Shapiro (ed) 'Man, Culture and Society' Oxford University Press, 1956

C Lévi-Strauss 'A World on the Wane' Hutchinson, 1961

B Malinowski 'The Sexual Life of Savages' Routledge, 1932

B Malinowski 'The Family among the Australian Aborigines' Schocken Books, 1963

O T Mason 'Woman's Share of Primitive Culture' Macmillan, 1895

M Mead 'Sex and Temperament in Three Primitive Societies' William Morrow, 1935

M Mead (ed) 'Cooperation and Competition among Primitive Peoples' McGraw-Hill, 1937

M Mead 'Some Theoretical Considerations on the Problems of Mother-Child Separation' American Journal of Orthopsychiatry 1954, XXIV, no 3

M Mead 'A Cultural Anthropologist's Approach to Maternal Deprivation' in M Ainsworth et al 'Deprivation of Maternal Care: A Reassessment of its Effects' Schocken Books, 1966

M Mead and N Newton 'Cultural Patterning of Perinatal Behaviour' in S A Richardson and A F Guttmacher (eds) 'Childbearing—Its Social and Psychological Aspects' Williams and Wilkins, 1967

G P Murdock 'Comparative Data on the Division of Labour by Sex' Social Forces, 1937, vol 15, no 4, p 551-53

G P Murdock 'Social Structure' The Free Press, 1965

R F Murphy 'Social Structure and Sex Antagonism' Southwestern Journal of Anthropology 1959, vol 15, no 1

National Manpower Council 'Womanpower' Columbia University Press, 1957

R Patai (ed) 'Women in the Modern World' (especially 'Sub-Saharan Africa' by E H Wheeler), Collier Macmillan, 1967

P Pinder 'Women at Work' Political and Economic Planning Broadsheet May 1969, 512

D Paulme (ed) 'Women of Tropical Africa' Routledge, 1963

A Scheinfeld 'Women and Men' Chatto & Windus, 1947

C G Seligman 'Races of Africa' Thornton Butterworth, 1930

A Storr 'Human Aggression' Pelican, 1970

E Sullerot 'Woman, Society and Change' World University Library, Weidenfeld, 1971

C Turnbull 'Wayward Servants' Eyre & Spottiswoode, 1965

M B Turner 'Women and Work' Institute of Industrial Relations, University of California, 1964

UNESCO 'Images of Women in Society' International Social Science Journal 1962, vol XIV, no 1

'United Kingdom Annual Abstract of Statistics' HMSO, 1969

B B Whiting (ed) 'Six Cultures' John Wiley, 1963

Woman's Bureau, Dept of Labour, Canada 'Women in the Labour Force in Nine Countries of Europe', 1962

CHAPTER 6

T Benedek 'Psychosexual Functions in Women' Ronald Press, 1952

M Diamond 'A Critical Evaluation of the Ontogeny of Human Sexual Behaviour' Quarterly Review of Biology 1965, 40, p 147-75

R B Edgerton 'Pokot Intersexuality: An East African Example of the Resolution of Sexual Incongruity' American Anthropologist Dec 1964, vol 66, no 6 pt 1

J L Hampson 'Determinants of Psychosexual Orientation' in F A Beach (ed) 'Sex and Behaviour' John Wiley, 1965

J L Hampson and J G Hampson 'The Ontogenesis of Sexual Behaviour in Man' in W C Young (ed) 'Sex and Internal Secretions' Bailliere, Tindall and Cox, 1961

W W Hill 'The Status of the Hermaphrodite and Transvestite in Navaho Culture' American Anthropologist Apr-Jun 1935, vol 37

D Levy 'Maternal Overprotection' Columbia University Press, 1943

P D MacLean 'New Findings Relevant to the Evolution of Psychosexual Functions of the Brain' in J Money (ed) 'Sex Research: New Developments' Holt, Rinehart & Winston, 1965

J Money 'Sex Hormones and Other Variables in Human Eroticism' in W C Young (ed) 'Sex and Internal Secretions' Bailliere, Tindall and Cox, 1961

J Money (ed) 'Sex Research: New Developments' Holt, Rinehart & Winston, 1965

J Money (ed) 'Psychosexual Differentiation' in J Money (ed) 'Sex Research: New Developments' Holt, Rinehart & Winston, 1965

R Stoller 'Sex and Gender' Science House, 1968

W C Young, R W Goy and C H Phoenix 'Hormones and Sexual Behaviour' in J Money (ed) 'Sex Research: New Developments' Holt, Rinehart & Winston, 1965

CHAPTER 7

L Ancona 'An Experimental Contribution to the Problem of Identification with the Father' in K Danziger (ed) 'Readings in Child Socialisation' Pergamon Press, 1970

R G Andry 'Delinquency and Parental Pathology' Methuen, 1960

U Bronfenbrenner 'Freudian Theories of Identification and their Derivatives' Child Development 1960, 31, p 15-40

D G Brown 'Sex Role Development in a Changing Culture' Psychological Bulletin 1958 vol 55, no 4, p 232-42

K Danziger (ed) 'Readings in Child Socialisation' Pergamon Press, 1970

W Emmerich 'Young Children's Discrimination of Parent and Child Roles' Child Development 1959, 30, p 405-19

L B Fauls and W D Smith 'Sex Role Learning of Five Year Olds' Journal of Genetic Psychology 1956, 89, p 105-117

S Freud 'Three Essays on the Theory of Sexuality' trans & ed J Strachey Hogarth Press, 1962

S W Gray and R Klaus 'The Assessment of Parental Identification' Genetic Psychology Monographs 1956, 54, p 87-114

R E Hartley 'Sex Role Concepts Among Elementary School Age Girls' Journal of Marriage and the Family 21 Feb 1959, p 59-64

R E Hartley 'A Developmental View of Female Sex-Role Identification' in B J Biddle and E J Thomas (eds) 'Role Theory' John Wiley, 1966

E M Hetherington 'A Developmental Study of the Effects of Sex of the Dominant Parent on Sex-Role Preference, Identification and Imitation in Children' in K Danziger (ed), Readings in Child Socialisation' Pergamon Press, 1970

H Holter 'Sex Roles and Social Structure' Universitetsforlaget, 1970

M Johnson 'Sex Role Learning in the Nuclear Family' Child Development 1963, 34, p 319-33

V Kidd 'Now you see said Mark' New York Review of Books 3 Sept 1970

L Kohlberg 'A Cognitive-Developmental Analysis of Children's Sex-Role Concepts and Attitudes' in E E Maccoby (ed) 'The Development of Sex Differences' Tavistock Publications, 1967

M B Loeb 'Social Role and Sexual Identity in Adolescent Males: a Study of Culturally Provided Deprivation' in G D Spindler (ed) 'Education and

Culture' Holt, Rinehart & Winston, 1963

K Lorenz 'The Childhood Genesis of Sex Differences in Behaviour' in J M Tanner and B Inhelder (eds) 'Discussions on Child Development' vol III Tavistock Publications, 1958

W Mischel 'A Social-Learning View of Sex Differences in Behaviour' in E E Maccoby (ed) 'The Development of Sex Differences' Tavistock Publications, 1967

H A Moss 'Sex, Age and State as Determinants of Mother-Infant Interaction' in K Danziger (Ed), Readings in Child Socialisation' Pergamon Press, 1970

L B Murphy 'The Widening World of Childhood' Basic Books, 1962

F I Nye and L W Hoffman (eds) 'The Employed Mother in America' Rand McNally, 1963

B Pasamanick, M E Rogers and A M Lilienfeld 'Pregnancy Experience and the Development of Behaviour Disorders in Children' American Journal of Psychiatry 1956, 112, p 613-18

J Piaget 'The Construction of Reality in the Child' Basic Books, 1954

M Rabban 'Sex-Role Identification in Young Children in Two Diverse Social Groups' Genetic Psychology Monographs 1950, 42, p 81-158

'Report of the Royal Commission on the Status of Women in Canada' (for 'Education and Stereotypes' p 173-187) Information Canada, 1970

R R Sears, E E Maccoby and H Levin 'Patterns of Child Rearing' Harper, 1957

CHAPTER 8

D J B Ashley 'Human Intersex' E and S Livingstone, 1962

B Bettelheim 'Symbolic Wounds: Puberty Rites and the Envious Male' Free Press, 1954

D Cooper 'The Death of the Family' Penguin Press, 1971

E Dahlstrom (ed) 'The Changing Roles of Men and Women' Duckworth, 1967

D L Dodge and W T Martin 'Social Stress and Chronic Illness' University of Notre Dame Press, 1970

M Duverger 'The Political Role of Women' UNESCO, 1955

M P Fogarty, R Rapoport and R Rapoport 'Sex, Career and Family' Allen & Unwin, 1971

A W Green 'The Middle Class Male Child and Neurosis' in A M Rose (ed) 'Mental Health and Mental Disorder' Routledge, 1956

H Hacker 'The New Burdens of Masculinity' Marriage and Family Living, August 1957, p 227-33

H F Harlow 'The Nature of Love' American Psychologist 1958, 13 (12) p 673-85

H F Harlow and M K Harlow 'The Effect of Rearing Conditions on Behaviour' in John Money (ed) 'Sex Research: New Developments' Holt, Rinehart & Winston, 1965

R E Hartley 'Sex Role Pressures and the Socialisation of the Male Child' Psychological Reports 1959, 5, p 457-68

R E Hartley and A Klein 'Sex Role Concepts Among Elementary School-Age Girls' Journal of Marriage and the Family 21 Feb 1959, p 59-64

R E Hartley 'Some Implications of Current Changes In Sex Role Patterns' Merrill-Palmer Quarterly 1960 vol 6, p 153-64

H Holter 'Sex Roles and Social Structure' Universitetsforlaget, 1970

J Itani 'Paternal Care in the Wild Japanese Monkey' Journal of Primatology 1959, vol 2, no 1

L Kanowitz 'Women and the Law: The Unfinished Revolution' University of Mexico Press, 1969

M Komarovsky 'Women in the Modern World' Little, Brown, 1953

P Lomas 'Childbirth Ritual' New Society 31 Dec 1964

F Lundberg and M F Farnham 'Modern Woman: The Lost Sex' Harper, 1947

K Millett 'Sexual Politics' Hart-Davis, 1971

L M Murphy 'The Widening World of Childhood' Basic Books, 1962

A Nemilov 'The Biological Tragedy of Woman' Allen & Unwin, 1932

A Oakley 'The Myth of Motherhood' New Society 26 Feb 1970

A Oakley 'Housewife: A Sociological Study of Domestic Labour and Child-rearing' (forthcoming)

E W Overstreet 'The Biological Make-up of Woman' in S M Farber and R H L Wilson (eds) 'The Potential of Woman' Man and Civilisation Symposium, McGraw-Hill, 1963

T Parsons 'Some Primary Sources and Patterns of Aggression in the Social Structure of the Western World' in his 'Essays in Sociological Theory' Free Press, 1954

A S Rossi 'Equality Between the Sexes: An Immodest Proposal' in R J Lifton (ed) 'The Woman in America' Houghton Mifflin, 1956

M Rutter 'Parent-Child Separation: Psychological Effects on the Children' Mental Health Research Fund, Sir Geoffrey Vickers lecture, 24 Feb 1971

R V Sampson 'The Psychology of Power' Pantheon, 1965

G Seward 'Sex and the Social Order' McGraw-Hill, 1946

E Sullerot 'Woman, Society and Change' World University Library, Weidenfeld, 1971

S S Tomkins 'The Biopsychosociality of the Family' in A J Coale et al 'Aspects of the Analysis of Family Structure' Princeton University Press, 1965

M Vaerting and M Vaerting 'The Dominant Sex: A Study in the Sociology of Sex Differentiation' Allen & Unwin, 1923

R J Williams 'Biochemical Individuality' John Wiley, 1956

M Yanowitch 'Soviet Patterns of Time Use and Concepts of Leisure' Soviet Studies 1963-4, vol 15, p 17-37

Acknowledgements

The author gratefully acknowledges permission to quote the following material:

Tavistock Publications for 'The Development of Sex Differences' ed. E E Maccoby; The Macmillan Co, New York, for 'Differential Psychology' by A Anastasi; University of Pennsylvania Press for 'The Criminality of Women' by O Pollak; Routledge & Kegan Paul for 'The Sexual Life of Savages' by B Malinowski; McGraw-Hill Book Co for 'The Potential of Woman' eds. S M Farber and R H L Wilson; Daedalus Journal for 'The Woman in America' ed. R J Lifton; The Society for Research in Child Development for 'Sex Role and Parental Identification' by D B Lynn; W B Saunders Co for 'Sexual Behaviour in the Human Female' by A C Kinsey et al; Longman Group for 'The Sexual Behaviour of Young People' by M Schofield; Penguin Books for 'Human Aggression' by A Storr; William Morrow & Co for 'Sex and Temperament in Three Primitive Societies' by M Mead; John Farquharson for 'Woman and Man' by A Scheinfeld; Eyre & Spottiswoode for 'Wayward Servants' by C Turnbull; Her Majesty's Stationery Office for 'Women of the Grassfields' by P Kaberry; Bailey Bros. for 'The Family among the Australian Aborigines' by B Malinowski; University of California Press for 'Comparative Data on the Division of Labour by Sex' by G P Murdock; Political and Economic Planning for 'Women at Work' by P Pinder; Science House for 'Sex and Gender' by R Stoller; The Williams and Wilkins Co for 'Sex and Internal Secretions' ed. W C Young; Harper & Row for 'Patterns of Child Rearing' by R R Sears, E E Maccoby and H Levin

The tables and figures are based on the following sources:

TABLES: (1) I B Weiner 'Psychological Disturbance in Adolescence' John Wiley, 1970; (2) G M Gilbert 'A Survey of Referral Problems in Metropolitan Child Guidance Centers' Journal of Clinical Psychology 1957; (3) L A DeLucia 'The Toy Preference Test: A Measure of Sex Role Identification' Child Development 1963; (4) H Barry, M K Bacon and I L Child 'A Cross-cultural Survey of Some Sex Differences in Socialisation' Journal of Abnormal and Social Psychology 1957; (5) F H McClintock and N H Avison 'Crime in England and Wales' Heinemann Educational, 1968; (6) H Hacker 'Women as a Minority Group' University of California Press, 1951; (7) W H Masters and V E Johnson 'The Sexual Response Cycles of the Human Male and Female: Comparative Anatomy and Physiology' in F A Beach (ed) 'Sex and Behaviour' John Wiley, 1965; (8) P H Gebhard, J Raboch and H Geise 'The Sexuality of Woman' Deutsch. 1970

FIGURES: (1) J Money 'Sex Research: New Developments' Holt, Rinehart & Winston, 1965; (2) C I Sandstrom 'The Psychology of Childhood and Adolescence' Penguin, 1966; (3) J W B Douglas and J M Blomfield 'Children Under Five' Allen & Unwin, 1958; (4) J Money 'Developmental Differentiation of Femininity and Masculinity Compared' in S M Farber and R H L Wilson (eds) 'The Potential of Woman' McGraw-Hill, 1963; (5) E Stengel 'Suicide and Attempted Suicide' Penguin, 1964; (6) A Anastasi 'Differential Psychology' Macmillan, New York 1958; (7) M Duverger 'The Political Role of Women' UNESCO, 1955